4XR: Developing Excellence in Reading

Nikki Gamble

Published by Just Imagine Story Centre Ltd

For more copies of this book, please email: info@justimaginestorycentre.co.uk

Tel: 01245 267748

Designed and set by Steven Woods

Printed in Great Britain by C3 Imaging print and graphics

Acknowledgement: This book is based on work undertaken in nine schools in the London Borough of Richmond. It would not have been possible without the hard work and dedication of the lead teachers who trialled and developed teaching approaches in their classrooms, and the participation and thoughtful feedback from their students. Thanks are due to the head teachers, staff and students at Barnes Primary School, East Sheen Primary School, Kew Riverside Primary School, Lowther Primary School, Richmond Park Academy, Sheen Mount Primary School, St Mary Magdelen's Catholic Primary School, St Osmund's Catholic Primary School, The Queen's School. We learnt so much from all of them. In particular, the following teachers have contributed case study material, exemplification of teaching and reflections on professional development and the process of change:

Mary Jane Blease
Debbie Canner
Judy Corry
Clare Durling
Camilla Garofalo
Scott Griffin
Theresa Guarino
Leanne Lisney
Suzanne Maille

Laura Martin
Rachel Marshall
Deborah O'Gorman
Marguerite Rodrigo
Carla Ruocco
Judy Shaw
Emily Treble
Kayleigh Squires
Rachel Wilson

Special thanks to consultant Ginny Germaney who efficiently maintained our records and data, coached the teacher researchers in schools and contributed to the film section to this guide.

Contents

CONTENT

Project Overview

4XR Developing Excellence in Reading project was set up to investigate the needs of high attaining students in years 6 – 8, to identify the most effective pedagogies to move learning on, and to increase attainment in reading. Within this frame of reference, the project sought to:

- cultivate teacher excellence and subject knowledge
- enable cross-school learning and a shared understanding of outstanding practice
- create new teaching resources to support ongoing professional learning
- further develop existing activities already tested and positively evaluated.

Project schools

The project was conducted in nine schools (eight primaries and one secondary) in the London Borough of Richmond from April 2014 – September 2015.

- Richmond Park Academy
- Barnes Primary School
- East Sheen Primary School
- Kew Riverside Primary School
- Lowther Primary School
- Mary Magdalene Primary School
- Saint Osmund's Primary School
- Sheen Mount Primary School
- The Queen's School

Expert teachers from each school were appointed as teacher researchers to work alongside consultants in order to develop and test ideas and strategies.

Project design

The project was conducted in eight phases:

- literature review
- baseline data collection
- gap analysis
- framework design
- training and development
- post-delivery data collection and analysis
- evaluation
- production of handbook and website.

Literature review

The literature review focussed on four inter-connected areas of relevance:

- reading comprehension
- dialogic teaching, including dialogic reading
- evidence based teaching strategies
- reading for pleasure and the development of a reading culture

A select bibliography can be downloaded at www.4XR.uk.

Baseline data

Data was collected using a battery of tools:

- teacher and pupil perception scales
- semi-structured interviews
- pupil focus groups
- observations of teaching using observation schedules and audio recording
- resource audits conducted in school libraries and classrooms
- reflective journal
- a standardised test (New Group Reading Test) was administered to years 6 and 7 in the project schools at the beginning and the end of the project.

The gap analysis

The gap analysis indicated that pedagogic approaches based on research, including work on reciprocal reading strategies, had been filtering into pedagogical practice. However, the following areas for further development were identified:

- increased knowledge and application of wider research
- wider and deeper subject knowledge including knowledge of quality texts
- appropriacy of intervention based on good assessment for learning.

Specifically, the following were highlighted as priorities:

- knowledge and understanding of the processes underpinning oral and reading comprehension
- teaching strategies to support comprehension, including inferencing and metacognition
- understanding of the effects of genre, syntax and vocabulary on reading comprehension
- knowledge of texts.

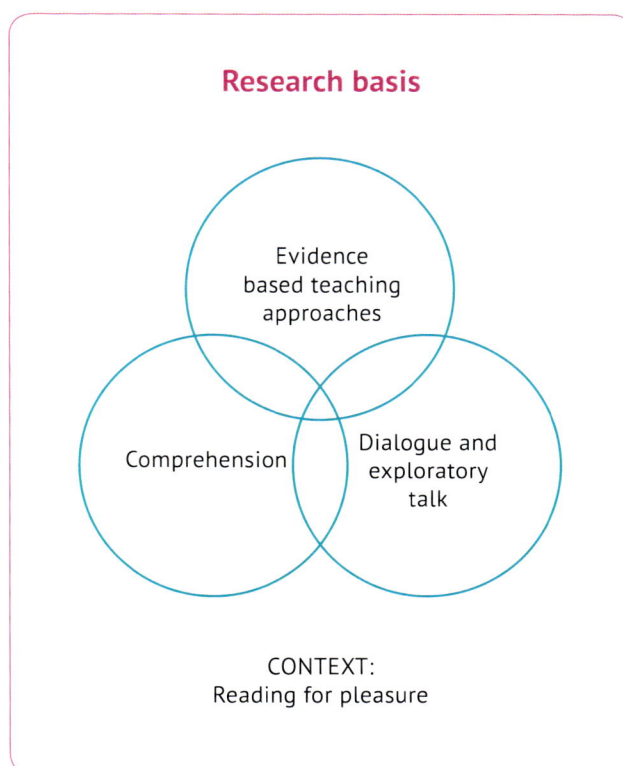

Research basis

Evidence based teaching approaches

Comprehension

Dialogue and exploratory talk

CONTEXT:
Reading for pleasure

4XR Framework

Framework

A flexible pedagogic framework was devised and introduced to teachers.

The 4XR learning and teaching cycle comprises five recurring stages. While there is a natural flow through each of these stages, they are not intended to be strictly linear. A cycle may have several smaller cycles within. A sequence may move through all stages in quick succession, or it may take several sessions to complete all stages. Furthermore, an activity can encompass more than one stage simultaneously, and the boundaries between stages may be blurred, as they are in some of our video exemplification. Nevertheless, taking account of the above, it is still helpful to look at how each of these stages works in concert with the others to deepen learning.

Excite

Excite is used here in the sense 'to get things moving', like water molecules in water that is being heated, rather than an 'all bells and whistles' introduction. In the opening moves of a session or sequence, teachers consider how the lesson will connect with students' prior learning, knowledge and interest. They may consider how to pique students' interest or evoke curiosity. The excite element can be a straightforward, low-key review of what has been previously learnt, or the creation of an exciting experience designed to provide background knowledge that will help the students access a challenging text.

Explore

Opportunities for students to explore their existing knowledge and understanding with their peers and with teachers. The exploratory stage allows students to examine and reflect on what they know and to organise and attach new learning to their existing schema. Creating opportunities for exploration, rather than moving too quickly to direct teaching, was one of the most significant changes in the 4XR project classrooms. An element of exploration allows teachers to make well informed judgements about students' understanding and misconceptions and consequently to intervene most effectively.

Expose

Using tools to expose and record students' thinking enables teachers to examine and reflect on what is known, and to plan next steps. Visual tools such as graphic organisers and Thinking Maps (David Hyerle) are particularly powerful in providing a sharper focus for in-line assessment, thereby potentially enabling teaching to begin at a higher level. For the higher attaining students in the 4XR project, the combination of exploration and the use of graphic tools to expose thinking led teachers to reflect on how these strategies had helped them to avoid 'underestimating what students can achieve.'

Expand

Having ascertained what students already know and what they are able to achieve independently, teachers identify next steps for learning. Scaffolded dialogue, guided work and interactive teaching are carefully structured to move thinking forward. Teachers make sophisticated judgements, ask questions, prompt and model speculation, rather than following a set of pre-determined questions. Collaborative work is important as a vehicle for allowing students to construct new understanding together. As they become increasingly independent and acquire metacognitive skills and strategies, they expand each other's thinking.

Review

The framework makes a distinction between reflection and reviewing learning. Reflection is ongoing throughout the learning process and accompanies active meaning making. Teachers are additionally encouraged to build in opportunities for focussed review at key points and at the end of a sequence, allowing students to explicitly reflect on the substantive content, the process of learning and the methods and organisation of learning.

Tools and strategies

A repertoire of associated tools and strategies was identified to be used in context with the process framework. These included:

- making good text choices and identifying the potential in texts

- developing effective questioning, including authentic self-questioning

- use of visual and graphic tools

- using reciprocal teaching strategies, but in a flexible framework rather than following a rigid sequence

- robust vocabulary instruction

- 'think alouds'

- inferencing strategies

- developing awareness of genre and syntactic features as they impact on comprehension

- substantive and process reflection.

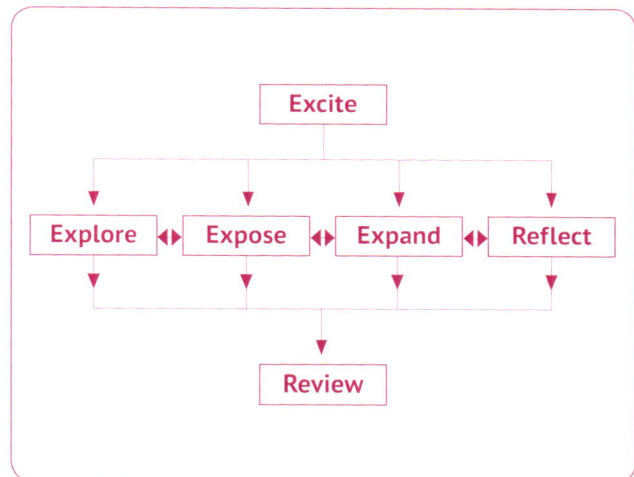

Reading Comprehension

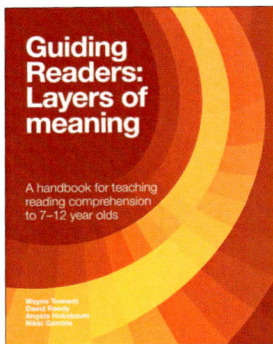

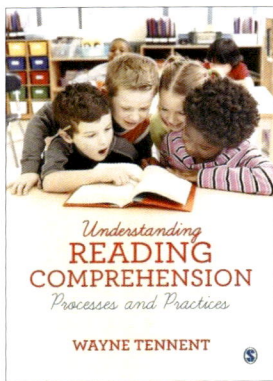

Guiding Readers: Layers of meaning

A handbook for teaching reading comprehension to 7–12 year olds

Wayne Tennent
David Reedy
Angela Hobsbaum
Nikki Gamble

Understanding **READING COMPREHENSION** *Processes and Practices*

WAYNE TENNENT

The major focus for this project was the teaching of reading comprehension and inferencing. In other words, the ability to make meaning from written and visual texts. Aligned with this are the skills of articulating understanding verbally and in writing.

A full bibliography is available on the website www.4xr.uk However, we draw teachers' attention in particular to Anne Kispal's literature review *Effective Teaching of Inference Skills for Reading* (2008) NFER which is a good introduction for teachers and subject leaders seeking to develop the teaching of reading comprehension. The report can be downloaded from the NFER website:

https://www.nfer.ac.uk/publications/EDR01/EDR01.pdf

An excellent text that helps to illuminate the processes of reading comprehension, especially inferencing, is Wayne Tennent's *Understanding Reading Comprehension*. For practical case studies and text suggestions, we recommend *Guiding Readers: Layers of meaning*. This is a useful text for the staffroom bookshelf.

The model of reading comprehension underpinning the 4XR project is a situational model derived from Kintsch and Rawson (2005). Fundamental to this model is the understanding that text comprehension is a complex process, requiring the involvement of many different components, working in concert as a system.

The model comprises three levels (the term *level* is used by Kintsch and Rawson with caution against the assumption that these processes are distinct and separate).

1. Linguistic: the reader recognises and processes individual words and their meanings. At the linguistic level a reader perceives and processes the graphic symbols on the page, recognises words. Parsing (the assignment of words to their role in a sentence) is an aspect of linguistic processing.

For example - drew = sketch, drag, pull out, attract, pull out at random.

2. Microstructure: work at sentence or phrase level in which the reader goes beyond words in isolation to recognise and process larger chunks of text.

For example - the chain he drew was clasped about his middle. It was long, and wound about him like a tail; and it was made (for Scrooge observed it closely) of cash-boxes, keys, padlocks, ledgers, deeds, and heavy purses wrought in steel.

The chain is something that is being worn, and drawn in this sense is likely to mean 'dragged along behind' as it is heavy.

3. Macrostructure: the reader recognises and processes themes, topics and genre information about the text.

For example - the same face: the very same. Marley in his pigtail, usual waistcoat, tights and boots. The chain he drew was clasped about his middle. It was long, and wound about him like a tail; and it was made (for Scrooge observed it closely) of cash-boxes, keys, padlocks, ledgers, deeds, and heavy purses wrought in steel.

Though he looked the phantom through and through, and saw it standing before him; though he felt the chilling influence of its death-cold eyes; he was still incredulous, and fought against his senses.

The reader starts to realise that the character's dress suggests this text may be set in the past or is perhaps taken from classic fiction. They may recognise the character, Scrooge, from Dickens' *A Christmas Carol*. There is an indication that this is a visitation from a ghost. The accoutrements of the phantoms' financial dealings appear to be weighing him down so that he is forced to remain earthbound.

Comprehension

What is evident from this model is that comprehension is the *outcome* of this complex processing system. This processing involves many components working together, including:

- world knowledge

- vocabulary knowledge

- processing sentence structure

- genre knowledge

- memory

- inference making

- comprehension monitoring.

And in consequence, as Tennent points out, comprehension cannot be taught. However, the skills needed for comprehension can be taught. The strategies used in the 4XR project target these component skills. They are:

- making connections

- thinking aloud and metacognitive strategies

- visualisation

- predicting

- questioning and question making

- summarising

- seeking clarification

- robust vocabulary instruction.

Further reading

Kispal, A. (2008) *Effective Teaching of Inference Skills for Reading*
Slough: NFER

Kintsch, W. and Rawson, K. A. (2005) Comprehension, in *The Science of Reading: A Handbook* (eds M. J. Snowling and C. Hulme), Blackwell Publishing Ltd

Tennent, W. (2015) *Understanding Reading Comprehension* London: Sage

Tennant, W., Reedy, D., Hobsbaum, A., and Gamble, N. (2016) *Guiding Readers: layers of meaning* London: UCL, Institute of Education.

RESOURCES

Selecting Texts

Andersen Press

> "
> *To teach reading comprehension well, teachers need to have a good knowledge and understanding of the texts they are using.*
> "

Choosing the right text

Choosing the right text is essential for developing reading comprehension. A multi-layered text will provide opportunities for the student to access it in different ways and will not limit the possibilities for interpretation and reflection.

Take one example: the Jeanne Willis and Tony Ross picture book *Tadpole's Promise*. On the surface, this is a straightforward 32 page picture book, a love story featuring a caterpillar and a tadpole who live in different environments and are destined to live apart; one in water, one in air. The caterpillar exhorts a promise from the tadpole that he will 'never change'. But of course it is a promise he is unable to keep. Each time he promises, he fails and eventually the tadpole turns into a frog. Of course, during the intervening period the caterpillar has also changed into a beautiful butterfly. The reader may hope that now the two can be together at least. But no, in a surprise twist, the frog leaps up and swallows the butterfly. It's an apparently simple tale. But delve a little deeper and it soon becomes apparent that the black marks on the page, the words, do not hold all the meaning. In order to appreciate the irony, the reader will need some knowledge of the real world; they will need to have some knowledge of metamorphosis to anticipate that the tadpole cannot keep his promise not to change, it goes against his very nature. When the story is read to very young children before they have yet acquired that knowledge, they will often be left perplexed at the end of the book and may ask, 'so where did the caterpillar go?' not realising that she has turned into the butterfly. This is one level in the story. But read a different way, one might see these characters not as a tadpole and a caterpillar but as a male and female engaging in an adolescent romance. It is a Romeo and Juliet story. This is love across the barriers between two young adults (no longer eggs but not yet fully formed adults) who love each other with intense but unrealistic passion. This interpretation of the story comes from a lived experience of human relations and from making connections with wider reading. Interpreting it this way isn't a prerequisite to understanding the story. Rather it can be understood differently by readers depending on their experience. However, the story has this capacity: it offers itself up for multiple interpretations. Using texts of this quality enables readers of different experiences and with different interpretative skills to access the text. There is room for growth and development.

Understanding the potential of the text

Early on in the project, teachers noted the challenges they faced in choosing quality texts that were appropriate and sufficiently challenging. To teach reading comprehension well, teachers need to have a good knowledge and understanding of the texts they are using. It is impossible to scaffold the learning without knowing the text and then understanding the meaning that the student is making from their reading. Making good interventions, prompts and questions arises from knowledge of both elements, the text and the reader.

We introduced a format for mapping the text's potential from Hobsbaum, Gamble, Tennant and Reedy *Guiding Readers* 2016. This flexible framework is intended to help the teacher read and identify aspects of the text that might be taught as well as features that might prove challenging to the readers. Once completed, the map can inform assessment and planning. The framework is not intended to be used as a fixed template. As the teachers became more experienced working with the diagram, they were able to adapt it to suit different texts and readers. See diagram on page 12.

Auditing resources

Auditing the resources available for teaching reading and for independent reading will help identify strengths and gaps. When auditing the stock, take into account texts available in the classroom and library. There may also be materials stored in cupboards that are rarely used. Is it because the texts are inappropriate or inaccessible? Surveying students' reading choices and their perceptions of reading at home and at school will also provide useful information that you can use to develop a strategy for resourcing reading.

What did our audits tell us?

Here are some insights that we have collated from the audits carried out in project schools:

1. Students equated challenging reading with progressing to longer books. The length of a book was viewed as a badge of honour, but generally the selections didn't offer challenges other than the stamina required to tackle the hefty tomes.

2. Texts used for group and guided reading were often too long, so students did not experience full texts, or lost momentum between sessions. Some of these books were much better suited to being read as a class novel or for independent reading.

3. There was an overuse of a limited number of authors and insufficient mapping of the range of writers that students would experience during the primary years.

4. Some text types were underused in guided and group reading. These included more challenging picture books, poetry, short story collections, non-fiction – including literary non-fiction.

5. There were few connections made between the texts and no evidence of bridging texts i.e. using a simpler text subject before moving to a more challenging text on the same theme or subject.

6. The selection of 'classic' texts was problematic. Teachers wanted to provide access to classic stories, but many of the books available to them were poor and cheaply produced adaptations which lacked child appeal.

See Appendix p78 Reading Audit

See Appendix p82 Pupil Perception Survey

RESOURCES

"
Auditing the resources available for teaching reading and for independent reading will help identify strengths and gaps.
"

Diagram Completed For *Tadpole's Promise*

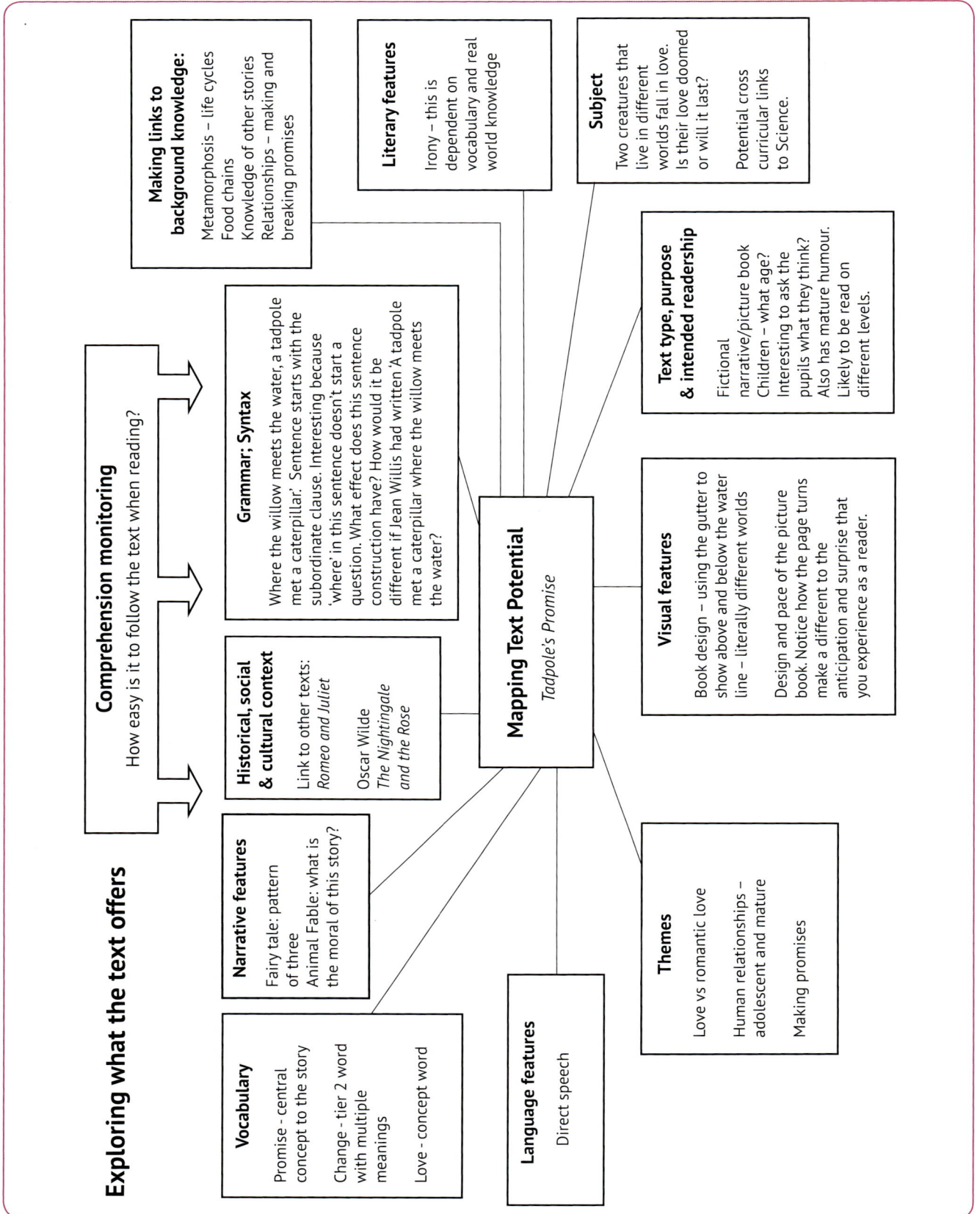

Exploring what the text offers

Comprehension monitoring
How easy is it to follow the text when reading?

Making links to background knowledge:

Metamorphosis – life cycles
Food chains
Knowledge of other stories
Relationships – making and breaking promises

Literary features

Irony – this is dependent on vocabulary and real world knowledge

Subject

Two creatures that live in different worlds fall in love. Is their love doomed or will it last?

Potential cross curricular links to Science.

Grammar; Syntax

Where the willow meets the water, a tadpole met a caterpillar.' Sentence starts with the subordinate clause. Interesting because 'where' in this sentence doesn't start a question. What effect does this sentence construction have? How would it be different if Jean Willis had written 'A tadpole met a caterpillar where the willow meets the water?

Text type, purpose & intended readership

Fictional narrative/picture book
Children – what age? Interesting to ask the pupils what they think? Also has mature humour. Likely to be read on different levels.

Historical, social & cultural context

Link to other texts: *Romeo and Juliet*

Oscar Wilde *The Nightingale and the Rose*

Mapping Text Potential

Tadpole's Promise

Visual features

Book design – using the gutter to show above and below the water line – literally different worlds

Design and pace of the picture book. Notice how the page turns make a different to the anticipation and surprise that you experience as a reader.

Narrative features

Fairy tale: pattern of three
Animal Fable: what is the moral of this story?

Vocabulary

Promise – central concept to the story

Change – tier 2 word with multiple meanings

Love – concept word

Language features

Direct speech

Themes

Love vs romantic love

Human relationships – adolescent and mature

Making promises

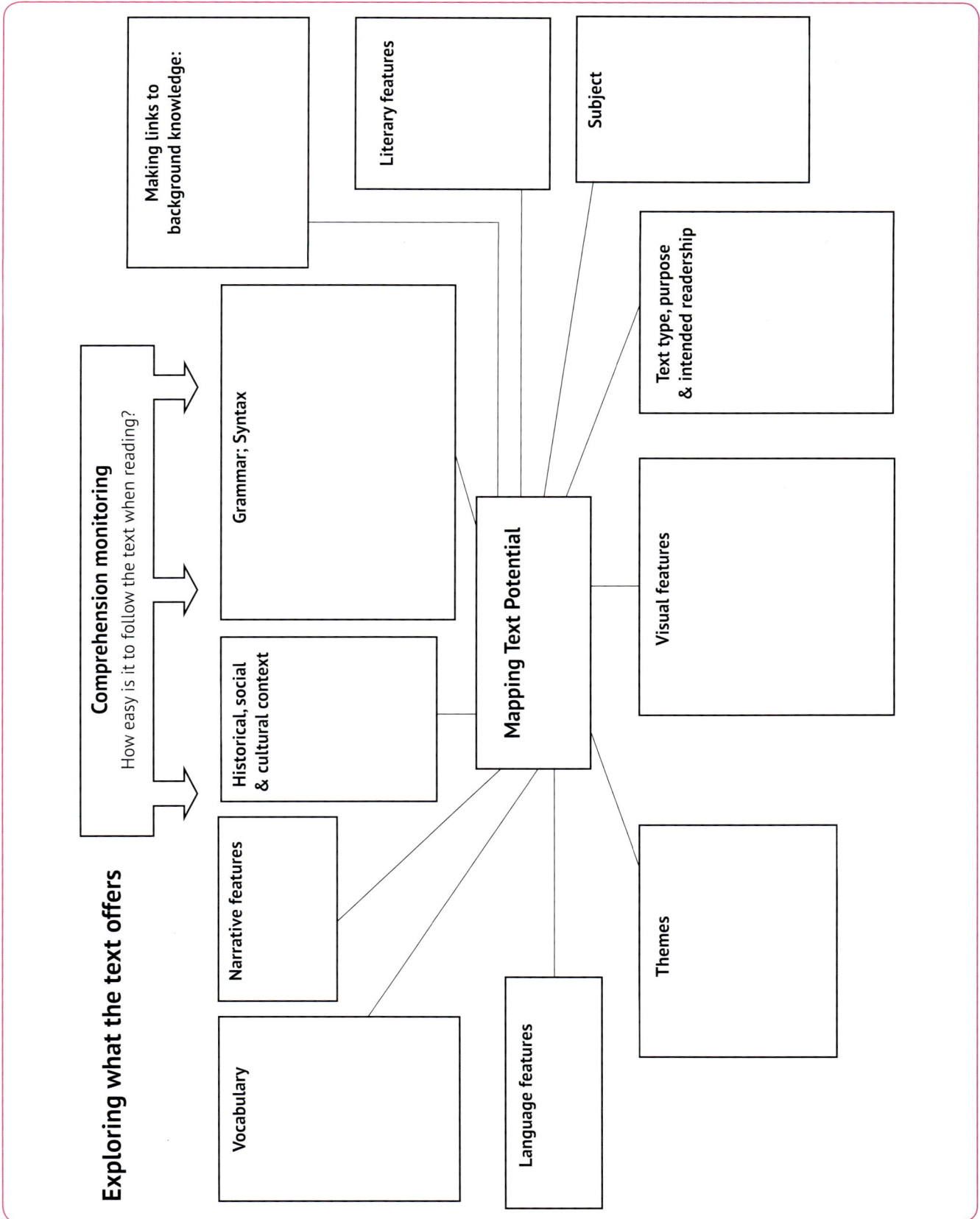

Exploring what the text offers

Comprehension monitoring
How easy is it to follow the text when reading?

Making links to background knowledge:

Literary features

Subject

Grammar; Syntax

Text type, purpose & intended readership

Historical, social & cultural context

Mapping Text Potential

Visual features

Narrative features

Vocabulary

Language features

Themes

Selecting Texts

What Works Well?

> " ... *tiny details can make very big differences to an interpretation of a text.* "

Picture books for older readers

As the example of *Tadpole's Promise* suggests, thoughtfully selected picture books can work with readers of all ages and levels of reading attainment. We found that many of the readers in our group that were considered 'high attaining' read quickly and equated progress with reading books of ever increasing length. This did not necessarily mean reading more widely, thoughtfully or with more sophisticated levels of understanding. Picture books require a different kind of reading, a slower-paced looking. Teachers working with picture books can make explicit the point that tiny details can make very big differences to an interpretation of a text. Although we had some reservations that capable readers and their parents might misunderstand why we were introducing picture books, our concerns were largely unfounded. Teachers noticed that the discussion about the picture books was more animated and inclusive. There were additional benefits too: although the project was mainly concerned with high attaining readers, working with picture books made it possible for groups of mixed reading abilities to access the same text and benefit from discussions.

Picture books often deal with challenging universal themes. The surreal imagery in Anthony Browne's picture books, *Gorilla*, *The Tunnel*, *Changes*, and *Voices in the Park*, reveal the psychology of his characters. David McKee's apparently simple *The Conquerors* deals with the most profound concerns about invasion, war and resistance. Armin Greder's *The Island* is a political fable as potent as George Orwell's *Animal Farm*.

Five great books for older readers

- Gary Crew & Shaun Tan - *Memorial*

- Jan Oke - *Major Glad and Major Dizzy*

- Tobhy Riddle - *Unforgotten*

- David Wiesner - *Flotsam*

- Graham Baker-Smith - *FArTHER*

Top tips for selecting picture books for older readers

1. Choose texts with deep and interesting themes for discussion.

2. Look for texts that employ interesting visual and verbal language.

3. Look at the ways in which the text and pictures work together. For example, plain text does not necessarily mean the book is simple. It may be used ironically when read alongside the pictures.

4. Make sure every child has their own copy – they do need to be able to explore at their own pace, as well as share ideas in the group.

Poetry

Poetry, with its compressed and richly allusive language, affords lots of opportunities for students to respond at many levels and to read between the lines. The length of a poem usually means that the whole text can be accessed in one sitting, although it may be returned to many times. Returning to a text after the students have started to process their thinking is really important as it allows them to build on initial thoughts and develop them further. Throughout the project we witnessed many epiphany moments when readers revisited texts.

From our audits we discovered that criteria for selecting poems was being driven by factors other than the quality of the poetry. Poems were mainly chosen to be used as models for writing. For instance Kit Wright's *Magic Box* was read, the structure analysed and then students wrote their own poems using that structure. We also found poems selected for their connection with curriculum topics. Often these 'curriculum poems' seemed to have be written expressly to fit with the curriculum. Consequently, many of the poems lacked depth and were too literal to generate much discussion.

A good poetry anthology will resource many lessons. Individual poems can be selected from the anthology to match the interests and needs of different groups.

Five super poetry books to update your collections

- Charles Causeley - *I Had a Little Cat*

- Chrissie Gittins - *Stars in Jars*

- Rachel Rooney - *My Life as a Goldfish*

- Gaby Morgan - *Poems from the First World War*

- Carol Ann Duffy - *A Laureate's Choice*

Top tips for selecting poetry

1. Have at least one set of a good anthology available in every classroom. This is excellent value for money when you consider how many lessons one anthology can support.

2. Make available a range of poetry for reading across the year regardless of the poetry students are writing: humorous, lyric, classic, modern, rhyming, non-rhyming, single poet collection, thematic collection etc.

3. Include poetry written for adults such as Ted Hughes' animal poems and classic narrative poems.

4. Make sure the newest poets are represented along with the well-established and the classic.

5. Keep an eye on the CLPE Children's Poetry Award shortlisted books. Buying a couple of sets each year will keep your collections up to date. www.clpe.org.uk

Five collections that shouldn't be forgotten

- Charles Causley - *Collected Poems for Children*

- Walter de la Mare - *Peacock Pie*

- Brian Pattern - *Utterly Brilliant Poetry*

- Kit Wright - *The Magic Box*

- Roger McGough - *Bad Bad Cats*

Selecting Texts

Five fantastic short story collections

- George Layton - *The Fib, The Swap, The Trick and Other Stories*

- Lari Don - *Winter Tales*

- Jamila Gavin - *Blackberry Blue*

- Michael Morpurgo - *Singing for Mrs Pettigrew*

- Rick Riordan et al - *Other Worlds*

Short story collections and shorter novels

Short fiction was often underutilised in the classrooms we worked in. The advantage of a short story is that it can be read in one or two lessons. It is easier for teachers to develop familiarity with shorter texts. Short stories avoid the problem of too many books remaining unfinished because there is insufficient time to read the entire book, or long gaps between sessions resulting in a lack of momentum and waning interest. Short stories such as Oscar Wilde's fairy tales may be a more digestible introduction to the classics than a longer novel and will help to familiarise students with the diction and register of pre-twentieth century text.

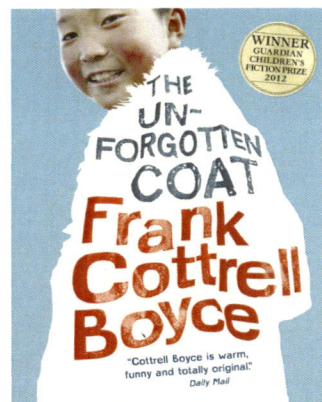

Walker Books

Of course short fiction doesn't entirely replace the need to read longer novels, which require readers to keep the plot in their heads over many different episodes as well as navigate the complexity of sub-plots. However, a mixed menu of shorter and longer texts planned across the year makes the organisation manageable and potentially more productive.

Furthermore, familiarity with short stories is likely to aid students' writing as the structure is more relevant to them at this stage than the more complex structures of novel writing.

Five short but powerful stories

- Frank Cottrell Boyce - *The Unforgotten Coat*

- David Almond and Dave McKean - *The Savage*

- Philip Pullman - *Clockwork*

- Russell Hoban and Alexis Deacon - *Jim's Lion*

- Malorie Blackman - *Cloud Busting*

Top tips for selecting short story collections

1. Include a range of classic and modern stories.

2. Be aware that not all stories in a collection will be suitable. We selected stories from *The Great War: an anthology of stories inspired by the First World War* with our year 6 groups, but there were some in the collection that we would not have read with them.

3. Some stories written for adults may be suitable too. We included stories by Ray Bradbury, Charles Dickens and Isaac Asimov in our workshops.

4. Choose stories that are well structured and with powerful themes that will elicit discussion.

Non-fiction

Our audits and observations indicated that non-fiction was used mainly for teaching the features of information texts, such as the use of structural guides (headings, captions) and index, contents and glossary. We saw non-fiction was used well to support individual and group research and to provide models for writing. However, opportunities to read non-fiction for pleasure and the discussion of non-fiction material was less evident. Non-fiction affords many opportunities to learn specialist vocabulary, to explore the way in which writers present a subject and indeed to explore the different ways in which a topic might be tackled in fiction and non-fiction. The same criteria for quality can be applied when selecting non-fiction.

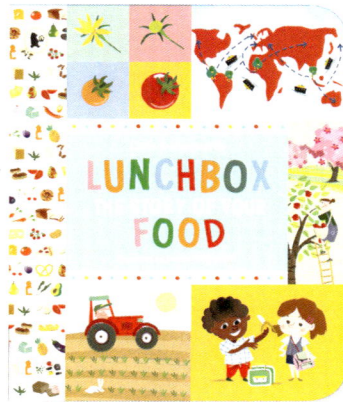

Walker Books

" *... explore the different ways in which a topic might be tackled ...* "

Top tips for selecting non-fiction

1. Is the subject presented in an interesting and logical way?

2. Is the language appropriate, challenging and lively?

3. Is it up-to-date and authoritative?

4. Non-fiction should be integrated into teaching across the curriculum, but also take the opportunity to read books about unusual, interesting and topical subjects. Connect with students' out of school interests and hobbies.

5. It is important to include a range of non-fiction: narrative non-fiction, photographic texts, information texts, newspaper articles, pamphlets etc.

6. Non-fiction is more than information and it can be designed and illustrated aesthetically. Look for imaginative forms of presentation and books written with an engaging voice.

Five non-fiction texts

- William Grylls
  - Shackleton's Journey

- Chris Butterworth
  - Lunchbox : The Story of Your Food

- Michaela Morgan
  - Walter Tull's Scrapbook

- Nicola Davies - *Tiny: The Invisible World of Microbes*

- Mick Manning and Brita Granstrom - *The Secrets of Stonehenge*

Selecting Texts

> " *Developing cine-literacy skills enables students to read, interpret and access the medium fully.* "

Film

Film is a powerful resource and focused or active viewing can enhance and develop the reading experience and hone students' critical skills. Developing cine-literacy skills enables students to read, interpret and access the medium fully. Furthermore, as film is generally a familiar medium for students, they may be able to access and understand techniques and devices, which can then be explicitly applied to reading. For instance, a year 5 group reading Grace Nichols' poem 'Forest' found it hard to comprehend that the forest in the poem is personified. They were sure that the poem was about a human being. The class then watched a selection of film clips in which objects and vehicles were personified such as Disney Pixar's *Cars* and *Beauty and the Beast*. This was followed by discussion about the status of the objects – was the candlestick a human or a candlestick? Why was it portrayed in this way? In the subsequent discussion the students demonstrated a clear understanding of personification which they were then able to apply when they reread Nichols' poem.

In parallel with the study of an author's written text, students can be guided to deconstruct, observe and analyse features — the contribution of light, sound, camera angles, colour and shape — in order to properly derive meaning. Comprehension then becomes most enjoyable by applying those skills to look deeper and discover more than they ever did before. As students gain confidence and experience, they can be challenged to extend their usual viewing repertoire to study film from different genres, eras and cultures. Discussions which compare the skills of authorial intent and directorial intent can also be very rich and rewarding.

Five great short films

- *Birthday Boy* – Korea 1951

- *Contre Temps* – a clock hunter makes a discovery in an apocalyptic underworld

- *Paperman* – Oscar winning silent romance

- *The Scarecrow* – Chipotle's hard-hitting fresh foods promotion

- *Hovis millennium advertisement* – 122 years of British history

Top tips for selecting and viewing films

1. Look for strong themes which have the potential to generate high quality discussion and debate, such as the value of friendship, overcoming difficulty, dealing with loss, love, war or racism.

2. A juxtaposition of emotions will lead to noteworthy differences in the way the aspects of film are used. For example, joyful and sad moments will lead to visual light and shade and changes in the soundtrack.

3. Vary students' cinematic diet by choosing from different genres and time periods. Older films are often visually dramatic and useful for comparison to modern features.

4. Watch the whole film before focussed work begins. This alleviates students' natural urge to know what happens next and supports the deeper analysis to follow.

5. View studied scenes several times in order to notice and capture more detail. This will better develop understanding of how production elements can be distinguished or brought together to convey meaning.

6. Ensure the film is suitable for the age range by checking on its certification through the British Board of Film Classification website. http://www.bbfc.co.uk/ To view films up to PG at the primary range, a permissions notice must be signed by parents. This is most often achieved through a whole school blanket agreement, as with internet use.

7. The charity-funded Into Film organisation and the linking Film Club site contain useful sources of film ideas split by topic and age range. http://www.filmclub.org/films

Five great feature films to use for developing comprehension

- Lemony Snicket's *A Series of Unfortunate Events*

- *Wall-E*

- *Nim's Island*

- *Corrina, Corrina*

- *The Spiderwick Chronicles*

Juxtaposing and comparing texts

When choosing texts it is useful to consider how texts can be connected. For instance, pairing a highly readable text with a more complex text dealing with similar themes and subjects produces a number of benefits. Firstly, readers can more quickly grasp the complex text than if it had been presented to them without this 'bridge'. Secondly, it reduces the need to keep moving on to new texts. Readers return to a previously read text to reconsider it in the light of subsequent reading.

> " ... *readers can more quickly grasp the complex text* ... "

Classroom activity

First we read and discussed Jeanne Willis and Tony Ross' *Tadpole's Promise*. Then we moved on to Oscar Wilde's *The Nightingale and the Rose*. These stories, written a century apart, may appear to be dissimilar but there are many points of connection. After reading and talking about each text separately we returned to *Tadpole's Promise* to see if there were any further insights as a result of reading the Wilde story. Some points of comparison included:

- Are there any similarities between the tadpole/butterfly and the student/professor's daughter?

- How do the endings of both stories compare?

- Do you think Jeanne Willis and Oscar Wilde have similar or different views about love?

- Do you notice any other connections between these two stories?

Both stories deal with the concept of 'romantic' love. Although the tone of the stories is different, they are both tinged with irony. Juxtaposing texts enables us to talk explicitly about making connections when we read, including the relationship of one text to another.

We witnessed some inspired pairings of texts in the lessons where it was evident that reading and discussing the first text had provided an orientation towards the second, more complex, text. We also found that after reading the second text the students refined their responses to the first text.

Five pairs of texts that produced thought provoking comparison

- Kevin-Crossley Holland - *Beowulf* & Wilfred Owen - *Dulce et Decorum Est*

- Kevin Crossley-Holland - *Beowulf* & Kevin Crossley Holland - *The Wild Man*

- Armin Greder - *The Island* & Ted Hughes - *The Iron Man*

- Gary Crew - *Memorial* and Michael Morpurgo et al - *The Great War*

- Meredith Hooper - *Ice Trap* & Thomas Hardy - *Convergence of the Twain*

Think Aloud

The Think Aloud strategy is used to encourage students to voice their internal thoughts as they read. Reading short units of text cumulatively, readers consider what individual words mean and how meanings shift and are firmed up as more information is provided. Students connect reading with their prior knowledge and complex thought processes are made visible.

Good teachers model thinking aloud, speculation and problem solving as part of their everyday teaching. The next step is to explicitly show students how they can use this strategy to monitor their own comprehension.

Here's an example of what a student Think Aloud looks like. The passage is taken from Charles Dickens' *A Christmas Carol*.

Walker Books

TEXT	The chain he drew
STUDENT	I think this person is an artist and he has just made a drawing of a chain around a lady's neck. Like a locket.
TEXT	was clasped about his middle.
STUDENT	Oh, that can't be right because this chain is clasped around is middle. Clasped is when you hold something.
TEACHER	Just hold, or is clasp more than hold?
STUDENT	It's when you hold it really tight, like gripped and this chain is round his middle like his waist. I think drawn means when you take something out like a sword, like this (makes a gesture as though drawing a sword from a scabbard) It could be that he's drawing the chain as though he is going to hit someone with it.
TEXT	It was long, and wound about him like a tail; and it was made
STUDENT	Yes, I think it's a big metal chain and is wrapped round him
TEACHER	Why is it like a tail?
STUDENT	I think it's because it's really long and it's dragging behind him like a tail. Or maybe it's because he looks half like a human and half like an animal.
TEXT	(for Scrooge observed it closely)
STUDENT	Oh, I know Scrooge. This is from our Christmas production, *A Christmas Carol*. I think it's Jacob Marley,
TEACHER	What do you notice about the punctuation?
STUDENT	It's in brackets. You say it like this (reads with expression). It's extra information in the sentence. It means that Scrooge is watching what's happening. He's looking really carefully.
TEACHER	Why do you think he is 'watching carefully'?
STUDENT	He's frightened and he isn't sure what it's going to do next. I think he might be horrified.
TEXT	of cash-boxes, keys, padlocks, ledgers, deeds, and heavy purses wrought in steel.
TEACHER	Remember to go back and read it from the beginning so you get a complete picture of what is happening.
STUDENT	The chain has got lots of things on it like keys and padlocks. I don't know what a ledger is. Deeds are things that you do like daring deeds but I don't think that makes sense. Everything IS made out of metal – steel.
TEACHER	A ledger is an account book. It's where you write down all the money that is paid to you and all the money you have to pay to someone else. Deeds are official documents that show that you own property, like the title deeds of your house or land. The piece of paper is proof that you own it
STUDENT	So his chain has lots of things attached to it. It's like a charm bracelet but all the things are really bad. They are all to do with money.

Think Alouds are used to model comprehension processes such as making connections with prior knowledge, predicting and visualising. In the example (opposite page) the student initially thinks that the chain is made out of metal and then confirms this when she learns that everything is wrought in steel.

Misconceptions become evident and assessment is facilitated as teachers listen in on student thought processes. Students articulate their ideas and teachers support their thinking by prompting e.g. 'is clasp more than hold?' or directing attention to bits of the text that appear to have been overlooked e.g. 'Why is it like a tail?'. Where appropriate, information is simply supplied e.g. ledger, deed.

Using the Think Aloud strategy

Think Aloud discussions need to be used analytically. It is important to model trial and error and speculative thinking. The teacher models language such as:

OK, so I will just re-read from the beginning to check what's going on here …

So far, I think I have learned that …

I don't understand what this bit means …

Ah, now I see why the author said … that makes sense now

This bit made me think of something I read … (or have seen, or happened to me)

I wonder why …

Once the students are familiar with the teacher using this type of thinking, they can begin to use Think Aloud working with a partner. One student (A) reads the text and (B) thinks aloud. They alternate with each section of text. Older students might take notes and record the processes their partner uses. Finally, they reflect on the learning process together.

Another way of using Think Aloud is to have individual students use the strategy when tackling a complex text. The teacher observes and makes notes of what the students are able to do independently and notes any particular challenges or difficulties.

Before, after and during reading

The Think Aloud strategy can be adapted and used at all stages of reading. In pre-reading the teacher might demonstrate accessing prior knowledge, or how to make informed predictions about the text. During reading, the focus may shift to demonstrate how individual words, syntax, punctuation and text structure affect how meaning is constructed. After reading, the emphasis will shift to how we look for evidence in the text to support opinions, weigh up an argument, or identify authorial point of view.

"

Misconceptions become evident and assessment is facilitated

"

STRATEGIES

Questions, Questions, Questions

> **"**
> *I think it has helped me with my understanding because now I stop when I finish a section of my reading and check I understand by asking myself questions.*
> **"**
>
> *Year 4 pupil*

Experienced and skilled readers ask lots of questions. By posing questions, voiced or internal, they monitor their own understanding and seek clarification.

Teaching approaches stemming back to the beginning of the last century might lead us to believe that comprehension develops as a consequence of being asked a series of questions that are posed by a knowledgeable student, someone who understands the true meaning of a text. You are probably familiar with the traditional comprehension exercise which looks something like this:

A short text or an extract is reproduced and followed by a number of questions. Typically the first questions are intended to be easier; these often require direct recall from the passage. The questions get progressively more difficult – or perhaps more interesting. The final question might ask the student to provide an opinion or evaluate the passage.

However, rather than facilitating comprehension, asking too many questions, verbal or written, in rapid succession, without giving students time to formulate their own thinking may have the opposite effect and inhibit comprehension.

From the moment pre-school children learn the meaning of the word 'why', they understand that they can use it to fulfil their desire for explanations. While parents may find the unending string of why questions a bit tiring and possibly even mildly irritating, students ask them not merely to extend conversation but to try and make sense, to comprehend their world. Part of the job of the teacher is to set up a climate in which this inquisitive quest for meaning flourishes rather than shuts down.

Questioning to 'get to the bottom of things' also applies to reading. This self-questioning arises in response to genuine curiosity or from seeking clarification in response to puzzlement or confusion. While a mature student will generate questions internally, often without a conscious awareness, less experienced students may need explicit support provided by teacher and peer models.

Questions, Questions, Questions

Effective questioning includes:

- Helping students formulate their own authentic questions and providing opportunities for them to pursue answers. The key word here is 'authentic'. Generating lists of questions without a genuine purpose or interest will be of limited value.

- Questions asked before, during and after reading. Since the late 1970s, research (Durkins, Pressley and others) has shown that questions asked before, during and after reading develop comprehension more effectively than only asking questions post-reading.

- Teacher asks questions which are responsive to pupil ideas and are structured to scaffold thinking, moving the student towards a clearer or deeper understanding of the text. Asking better questions is not simply using a range of different question types. Although teacher awareness of question types can help move teachers away from habitually asking a narrow set of questions, it is even more essential to apply that knowledge appropriately, through judicious choice in context. Teacher questions that arise out of dialogue with students will more successfully move students' understanding on, rather than a prepared checklist of questions, which focuses on coverage rather than the students' needs.

" ... questions asked before, during and after reading develop comprehension more effectively ... "

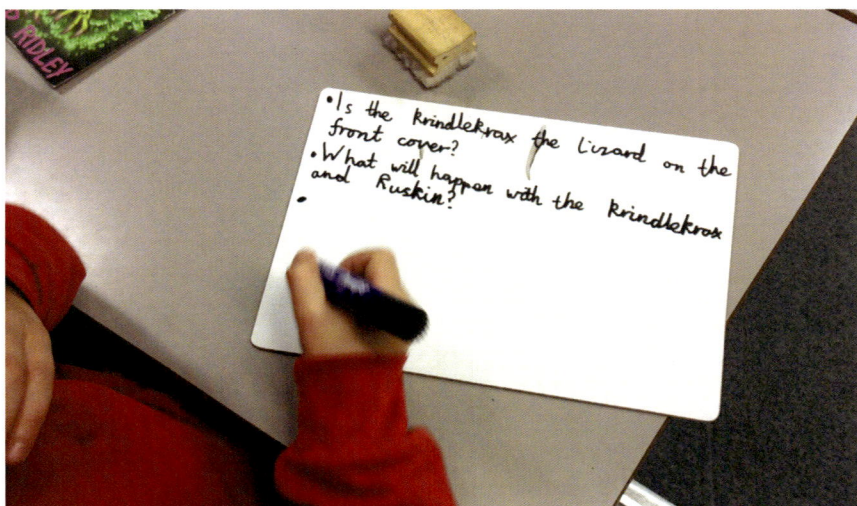

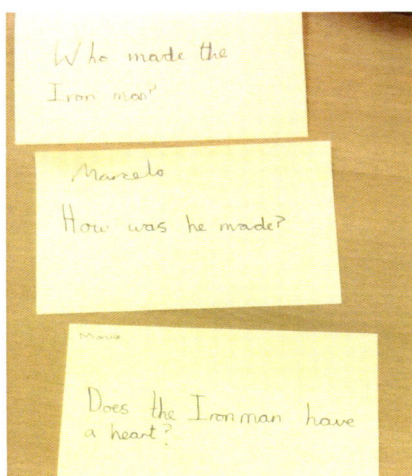

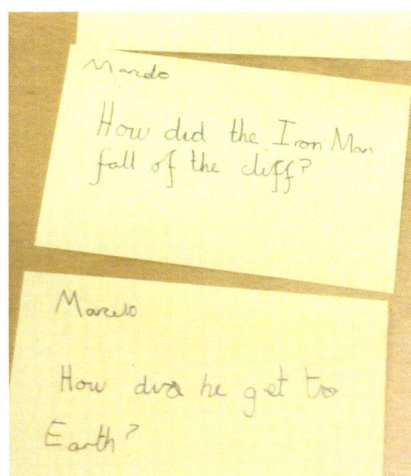

Questions, Questions, Questions

> *The types of question that we might ask before, during and after reading support the reading process at each stage rather than test the reader on their recall.*

Learning how to ask questions

Students learn how to ask questions when teachers model the questioning process.

Before reading

Questions might include:

- What are the clues that tell me what kind of text this is?

- Is this going to be a factual or a fiction text?

- Can I trust the author of this text (reliability of the source)?

- What do I already know about this subject?

- What predictions can I make about what is going to happen in this story?

- What clues does the title give me about the story?

- Have I read any other books by this author? Do I have any expectations for the type of story this author writes?

During reading

Plan to stop at convenient points to pose questions such as:

- What is the main idea in this text?

- What do I understand at this point?

- Do I need to reread this paragraph to clarify my understanding?

- Are there any words that I need to define to help me understand this text?

- What pictures of the setting are being created in your head in this first chapter of *The Dark is Rising?*

After reading

Ask questions to encourage students to think about text choices or conjecture the author's intentions:

- Why do you think Anthony Browne chose to show only the back of the girl's head in the final picture in *The Tunnel*?

- Why do you think Oscar Wilde chose to end *The Nightingale and the Rose* in this way?

- Whose idea of love do you think Oscar Wilde considered to be most true: the nightingale's or the student's? What evidence can you find in the text to support your ideas?

- Why do you think Shaun Tan chose this setting for *The Lost Thing*?

- Why do you think Charles Causley chose to use the word 'family' in his poem Maggie Dooley?

- Why do you think Jeanne Willis chose a tadpole and a caterpillar as characters for her story *Tadpole's Promise*?

- Why do you think David Almond chose Michael as the narrator for *Skellig*?

Questions, Questions, Questions

Prompts to help students formulate questions

After modelling different types of questions, provide a set of prompts to reinforce the idea of asking questions before, during and after reading. These can be reproduced on strips of card and used as bookmarks. The prompts can be adapted for different types of text and more challenging questions used as the students' proficiency and confidence increases.

Before reading

- What clues does the title give about the type of text?

- What type of text is it?

- Fiction? Non-fiction? Poetry?

- Are there clues to the genre? e.g. mystery, adventure.

- Do I already know anything about this subject?

- Have I read any other books by this author?

- Can I make any predictions about this text?

During reading

- Have I understood what I have just read?

- Is there anything that I find strange/puzzling/confusing?

- Would it help if I reread this paragraph/page/chapter?

- Can I identify the main idea?

- Can I summarise the page/ chapter I have just read?

- What pictures do I get in my head from reading this page/ chapter?

- Are there any words that I don't understand? Do I need to know them to understand the text?

After reading

- Did the text remind me of anything e.g.
  - other books that I have read
  - films that I have seen
  - things that have happened to me
  - something that I have heard about

- Were any of my predictions confirmed?

- Were there any surprises?

- What were the main ideas and themes in this text?

- Why did the author:
  - choose this setting?
  - choose to end the story in this way?
  - choose this point of view?

Questions, Questions, Questions

> *Last year when we read a book, we would read it and then answer some questions set by the teacher. However now that we get to ask our own questions, I think more about what the book has said and its meaning.*

Year 4 pupil

> *Question organisers are useful tools for assessing progress when revisited periodically. You can see which questions the students are able to answer and record new questions as they arise from discussion.*

Year 5 teacher

Using question organisers

Question organisers can be used to help students analyse their own questions and also to help the teacher identify the most productive next steps for teaching.

For example a Question Quadrant like the one below can be used to plot questions that the students have posed at the end of reading a text:

	Answer in the text	Answer not in the text
Only one potential answer		
More than one potential answer		

To demonstrate the process, the teacher works with some of the students' questions to make explicit the decision making process. The aim isn't to find answers at this stage, though inevitably there will be some discussion about likely answers while completing the activity.

After modelling, the students will be able to complete the grid independently. When all the questions have been plotted on the grid, the students can reflect with the teacher about why they chose to put particular questions in each of the boxes. Were some more difficult to decide than others? Why? The allocation of some questions to boxes will be obvious but others will be difficult to determine. However, it is the analytical discussion that is important rather than the box filling and it is fine to have some uncertainty.

The Question Quadrant is a flexible tool which can be used in a number of ways depending on your aims for the students learning. For instance:

- a group might complete a question quadrant at the end of a group discussion but prior to a guided reading session with the teacher. The quadrant can then be used by the teacher to plan the guided session

- the teacher can identify the question that is likely to lead to the most productive discussion and use that to open the guided reading lesson

- the teacher might look for the questions that haven't been asked. Is there something obvious missing? Is this because the students haven't fully understood the text or have they overlooked something important. The guided session might start by exploring why that question wasn't asked

- the students can revisit the text independently and after rereading, delete the questions that they have managed to answer themselves. Answers can be added. To chart the students' thinking across a sequence of lessons, use different coloured pens on different days. In this way you will be able to see which questions they have answered. When students revisit the text, some questions will be answered but further questions may arise, taking the thinking even deeper. Ask students to record the new questions using a different colour. Giving students time to revisit their questions allows them to take more ownership of the process and leads to deeper learning. It places an emphasis on careful listening to each other's contributions and the development of critical argument as they learn to respectfully agree and disagree with each other's ideas.

Questions, Questions, Questions

The questions raised and recorded by year 6 students at reading *Memorial* by Gary Crewe and Shaun Tan

	Answer found in the text	Answer not found in the text
Question has one answer	• When did Issy Jacobs die? • What type of tree was it? • What did little Philly Whipps lose his leg to?	• Why are some of the pictures in black and white?
Question has more than one answer	• Where was the tree planted? • Who was the tree planted for?	• Why did they choose to plant a tree? • Why do some of the pictures reflect childhood? • Why is there a reflection of soldiers in the water when there are none? (Illustration page 11)

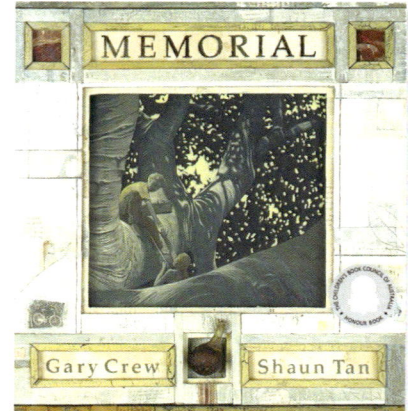

Hodder Children's Books

And this example was completed by year 5 students after reading *Flotsam* by David Wiesner

	Answer found in the text	Answer not found in the text
Question has one answer	• Why is the book called Flotsam?	• Is this beach a real place that the author knows? • If the girl at the end developed the film, what would she see? • Is it the boy's imagination or is it real?
Question has more than one answer		• Why didn't the boy show anyone the photos? • Why are all the photos of children and no adults?

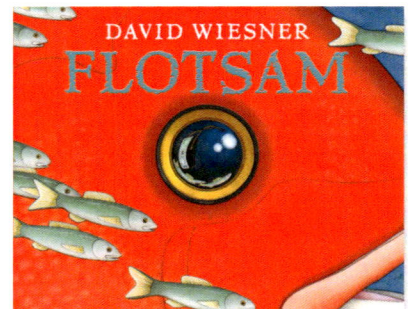

Andersen Press

See Appendix, p86 for photocopiable Question Quadrant

Questions, Questions, Questions

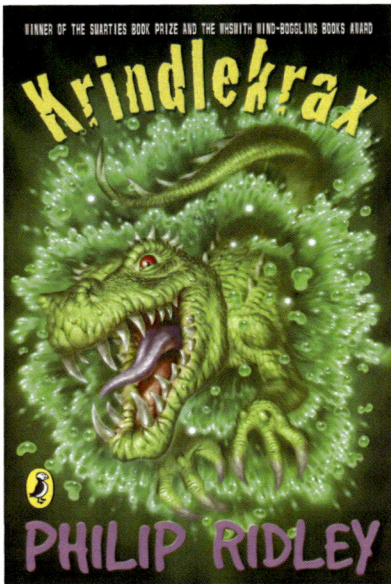

Question organiser for *Krindlekrax* by Philip Ridley

Working across two sets of conditions might be too difficult for younger students. In one year 4 class the teacher came up with a solution to simplify the process. She decided to use just two boxes and one large question organiser was used for the whole class. The students wrote questions on post-it notes and placed them on the organiser. As they read further, they returned to it and removed the questions that they had answered. As the class read further, new questions were added as they arose.

Questions where there can be only one answer:

- Why did Corky get a medal?

- Is Lizard Street named after Krindlekrax?

- Did Corky create Krindlekrax?

- Is the Krindlekrax a mutant?

- Do Ruskin's parents know about the Krindlekrax?

Questions where there can be more than one answer:

- How does Corky know about Krindlekrax?

- Why does the Krindlekrax live in the sewers under Lizard Street?

- Will Ruskin get to meet Krindlekrax?

- How does Ruskin feel about Corky telling him about the Krindlekrax?

> "
> *It's helped my comprehension because whenever we read a chapter we recap on it and we talk about it and ask questions and go back and answer questions we have asked before.*
> "
>
> *Year 4 pupil*

Do Ruskin's parents know about the Krindlekrax?

Top tip

Encourage the students to write their questions on post-it notes which can then be collected and presented together on the organiser.

Questions, Questions, Questions

Question organiser for *How to Live Forever* by Colin Thompson

This was extended to the analysis of questions where the answers could be found or could not be found in the book. The students discovered that some of the questions that they asked were not specific to the book. These 'Text to World Questions' (Keene and Zimmerman, 1997) are called General Questions on the question organiser below:

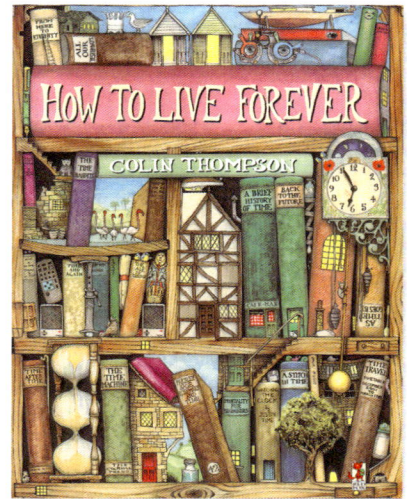

Red Fox

Questions that we could answer from the book:

- How did the book vanish?

- Did the book vanish by itself or did someone take it?

- Why was it that particular book was stolen?

- Has the person who stole the book lived forever?

- Is the person who hid the record card an important person in the book?

- Does each book house a spirit?

Questions which we were unable to answer from the book:

- Did someone who worked there steal it?

- Was it stolen because it was a popular book?

....

General questions:

- Why would someone want to live forever?

> "
> *Students answering their own questions rather than mine makes them active rather than passive readers. It has created a community of readers who see and value the importance of asking questions as readers.*
> "
>
> *Camilla Garofalo,*
> *Barnes Primary School*

✏ Classroom activity

Introduce question organisers to a class or group. After the students have used the organiser to map their questions, reflect on the questions they have asked:

- Which questions will be easiest to answer?

- Is there one question that strikes you as having potential for framing a subsequent guided reading session (i.e. teacher-led session)?

- Are there any questions that could be pursued as a homework task?

- Are there surprising omissions i.e. did you expect them to ask a question that wasn't asked?

- How will you use the question quadrant to chart student progress through a sequence of work?

Questions, Questions, Questions

Quescussions

One way to encourage students to question as they read is to have a discussion which is conducted entirely through questions. This technique is called a Quescussion and was developed by Paul Bidwell at the University of Saskatchewan. Quescussions are usually short (around two to five minutes) but are governed by the interest of the group and the rate at which the questions are asked. Initially there may be some silences and it is important to allow thinking time rather than step in too quickly.

One of the benefits is that because contributions are short, students who may be reluctant to talk in class feel more comfortable to volunteer a question. Quescussions encourage more experimental and creative thinking because they are tentative. The teacher takes on the role of scribe to record the questions. These can then be grouped and organised and presented back to the class for future discussion.

A few simple rules are required for the success of a Quescussion:

- the discussion can only contain questions

- the teacher may stop the Quescussion to help the students think about the type of questions they are asking. They may be encouraged to ask more open-ended questions e.g. Why? What? How? They might be encouraged to ask questions about feelings, if only factual questions are being asked. They might be encouraged to ask simple knowledge questions, for instance about the meaning of words

- a pupil who asks a question must wait until at least four other questions have been asked before asking another

- questions are asked without the need to raise hands. The teacher only intervenes if more than one pupil speaks at the same time

- if a statement is made instead of a question the whole class will say 'STATEMENT'. It may be possible to rephrase the statement as a question.

Here's an example taken from a year 6 Quescussion about a passage from *The Secret Garden*. This passage was given to the class to read prior to them starting to read the novel. The Quescussion enabled the class to ask many of the questions that are central to understanding the behaviour of Mary Lennox.

Mary had liked to look at her mother from a distance and she had thought her very pretty, but as she knew very little of her she could scarcely have been expected to love her or to miss her very much when she was gone. She did not miss her at all, in fact, and as she was a self-absorbed child she gave her entire thought to herself as she had always done. If she had been older she would no doubt have been very anxious at being left alone in the world, but she was very young, and as she had always been taken care of, she supposed she always would be. What she thought was that she would like to know if she was going to nice people, who would be polite to her and give her her own way as her Ayah and the other native servants had done?

She knew that she was not going to stay at the English clergyman's house where she was taken at first. She did not want to stay. The English clergyman was poor and he had five children nearly all the same age and they wore shabby clothes and were always quarrelling and snatching toys from each other, Mary hated their untidy bungalow and was so disagreeable to them that after the first day or two nobody would play with her. By the second day that had given her a nickname which made her furious.

Frances Hodgson Burnett *The Secret Garden*

Who is Mary?

Why is she sent to the clergyman's house?

Has her mother died?

Why doesn't it mention her father?

How old is Mary?

Why is she self-absorbed?

What does self-absorbed mean?

Why does she only see her mother from a distance?

Why is she going away?

Why is she horrible to the clergyman?

Where does Mary live?

What is an Ayah?

Where is this story set?

I think it's set in India - STATEMENT

Is it set in India?

When is it set?

Who wrote this story?

Why does she have servants?

Is Mary rich?

Why is she alone in the world?

What nickname do the other children give Mary?

Why doesn't she like the clergyman's children?

She's posh and stuck up - STATEMENT

What does disagreeable mean?

Where will Mary go next?

Questions, Questions, Questions

✏ Classroom activity

- How would you group the questions from this Quescussion?

- Identify a question that you think could be used to focus subsequent discussion. It could be a question that you return to several times during the reading of the novel.

- Which questions are likely to be less important for the rest of the novel?

> *"*
> *Quescussions encourage more experimental and creative thinking because they are tentative.*
> *"*

In this Quescussion year 4 students asked questions about a photograph showing two girls on board a ship.

Who are these girls?

Are they sisters?

Are they friends?

Are they on a ship?

Where are they going?

Where are they leaving?

Is it a long voyage?

Is it hot?

What is she holding?

Is it a toy?

Why are they sad?

Who took the photograph?

Will they get there safely?

Where are their parents?

Will they stay together?

Are they alone?

Is it a holiday?

Do they want to stay or do they want to go?

Why is the photograph called Bon Voyage?

Questions, Questions, Questions

> *Making a statement, on the other hand (especially a declarative one) can alter the dynamic and reinvigorate the discussion.*

Statements: an alternative to questions

Asking direct questions isn't the only way to encourage pupil questioning. In fact too many direct questions can feel interrogative and off putting. Many teachers will have at some point experienced a class or group responding with blank faces and silence to a raft of questions. Even when it isn't intentional, questions can feel like an examination. Making a statement, on the other hand (especially a declarative one) can alter the dynamic and reinvigorate the discussion. Initially students may need to have it explained that such statements are an invitation for discussion and are not incontrovertible.

A group of 4XR students were recently taking part in a discussion about an author visit they had just had, with the intention of gaining an insight into the value that they placed on the experience. The question was posed, 'Do you think it is important that authors visit schools and talk to students?' Most agreed that it was but didn't offer further explanation. This was followed up with a supplementary question, 'Can you tell me why you think that?'. The responses were short and not very illuminating. A different tack was tried using a statement, 'It's really easy these days for authors to make videos, which you can watch in the classroom. Author visits aren't necessary because you can get all the information you need on the internet.' At this point there was an animated refuting of the statement that been made:

Pupil: It's not the same.

Teacher: But you can learn exactly the same things from a video.

Pupil: But you couldn't make a giant squid (the author had invited volunteers from the class to demonstrate the size of one of the monsters in his book).

Teacher: Is that important?

Pupil: Yes because we can get involved. You can't do that with a video.

Pupil 2: It feels really special, we have read the book and now the author is here speaking to us ... it's just for us and we can ask whatever we want to.

Questions will arise naturally in the discussion that follows when statements are posed. Rather than looking for the 'right' answer, students start to question what the statement means and to find evidence to prove or disprove it. This is especially the case when strong statements, which allow for differing points of view and contention, are presented. To develop reading comprehension, statements should be constructed in a way that require the students to return to the text in order to refine their understanding.

Some example statements:

Gary Crewe and Shaun Tan - *Memorial*	'People's memories are more important than memorials.'
Oscar Wilde - *The Nightingale and the Rose*	'Oscar Wilde thinks education is more important than love.'
Charles Causley - 'Maggie Dooley' (poem)	'Maggie Dooley is lonely and unloved.'
Homer - *The Odyssey*	'In The Odyssey vengeance is valued more highly than forgiveness.'
Anthony Browne - *The Tunnel*	'The boy is braver than the girl.'
William Shakespeare - *Romeo and Juliet*	'Romeo and Juliet is more comedic than tragic.'

"
Rather than looking for the 'right' answer, students start to question what the statement means ...
"

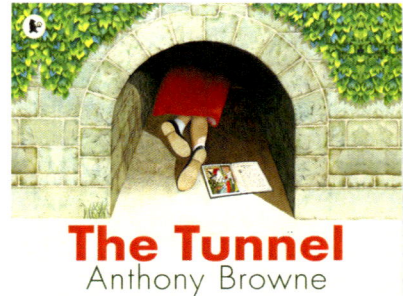

The Tunnel
Anthony Browne

Red Fox

Suggestions for using statements to replace questions in your teaching:

- When you feel you are asking too many questions and want to inject more vigour into the discussion, reformulate your questions as statements and see if it makes a difference.

- Give groups a number of statements on cut out strips of paper and ask the students to determine whether they agree or disagree with the statements or whether they are undecided. When they have considered their evidence they position the statements on a prepared grid, and provide evidence from the text to support their choice. For non-fiction texts it may be more appropriate to use the words true, untrue, unsure.

Top tips for writing statements

- Identify themes, characters, plot dilemmas which allow for multiple perspectives or might be puzzling and benefit from closer reading

- Express statements simply and concisely

- If writing multiple statements include some contradictory statements

Questions, Questions, Questions

An example using statements about Anthony Browne's *Gorilla*

Agree	Disagree	Undecided	Reasons
		Hannah prefers spending time with the gorilla to spending time with her father.	Hannah looks much happier when she is with the Gorilla. The pictures with Hannah and her father look colder and less friendly. Hannah would rather spend the time with her father but he doesn't have time for her. His is too busy or thinking about other things.
	Hannah's father enjoys work more than he enjoys spending time with Hannah.		Hannah's father is always working but he doesn't look very happy. It doesn't look as though he is enjoying his work. It looks as though he works because he has to. The story doesn't mention Hannah's mother. Perhaps her father has to work to earn enough money for them to have a house and food.
Hannah is lonely			Hannah is pictured alone in her room. She is shown in the corner looking small. Her body language shows that she is unhappy. She has nobody to play with and her father doesn't even notice her at breakfast.

- Give a group a strong statement and ask them to discuss. Record or observe their discussion, making note of any questions they ask. A teacher or teaching assistant can observe this discussion and note any key questions that arise. These can then be used to initiate a structured whole class discussion.

- Once students are used to working with statements invite them to write statements for other groups to discuss. Discuss the difference between weak and strong statements i.e. those that have a single correct or obvious answer and those that require more thought and have more than one potential answer.

Reflection takes place incidentally throughout the learning. The purpose is to encourage students towards self-determination, to encourage responsibility for their own learning, to enable them to see the value in the learning that has taken place, to understand what makes things challenging and also worth the effort. Through reflection students acquire new learning skills; they learn how to learn. They also learn how to identify personal learning goals.

Reflection after reading

There are several ways students can be encouraged to reflect at the end of a sequence of work:

- thinking, learning or process journals in which students review their learning journey

- revisiting and annotating tools used earlier in the process in order to chart the learning journey. For instance, a question quadrant constructed at the outset can be revisited with annotations made using coloured pens to show that questions have been answered or partially answered. Further questions might be added, demonstrating that asking questions is an ongoing process rather than finite

- group or class discussion using substantive and procedural prompts.

" Through reflection students acquire new learning skills; they learn how to learn "

Substantive reflection prompts

- Did we achieve our goals?

- Did we come up with good ideas and fruitful suggestions?

- Did we examine the main themes in this story?

- How good were our reasons for supporting what we said?

- Did we deepen our understanding of significant ideas?

- Are there any outstanding issues that need resolving?

- Where could we take this discussion next?

Procedural reflection prompts

- Did we listen well?

- Did we build on one another's ideas?

- Did we explore our disagreements?

- Did everyone have an opportunity to contribute?

- Did you learn anything new from another student?

Vocabulary and Reading Comprehension

The connections between vocabulary acquisition and reading comprehension

The correlation of vocabulary knowledge and reading comprehension is widely accepted and has been demonstrated in numerous research studies (Singer 1965, Carroll 1993, National Reading Project 2000 and others). Young students acquire vocabulary orally and this plays a part in their early reading. In the beginning stages of reading, students encounter words which they may not have seen written down that are, however, already part of their oral vocabulary. As a result of prior knowledge, they are more likely to understand what they read. It follows that the more extensive a reader's oral vocabulary, the easier it will be for them to make sense of text. Furthermore, early vocabulary knowledge is a predictor of reading comprehension in older students (Cunningham and Stanovich 1997 and others).

Once students have acquired independence and fluency in their reading, written text replaces oral language as the primary source for encountering new words. Proctor et al (2012) concluded that vocabulary instruction was significant for students beyond the beginning stages of learning to read and therefore of particular interest to the 4XR framework.

Vocabulary breadth and depth

There are two elements to vocabulary knowledge:

- breadth being the number of words that a student knows

- depth being the extent of the knowledge that a student has about a specific word including its relation to other words and knowledge of its structure.

Research studies have shown that breadth and depth of vocabulary are both predictive of reading comprehension, particularly the ability to make inferences (Oakhill and Cain, 2014). Oulette (2006) argues that deep level knowledge has a greater impact on comprehension and that it is less beneficial to know lots of words more superficially. Our observation of vocabulary teaching in the project schools indicated a concentration on increasing the breadth of vocabulary but a weaker focus on depth. We return to this point in the recommended teaching approaches outlined below.

Continuum of word knowledge

Vocabulary development is cumulative. A continuum of word knowledge outlined by Beck et al serves as a reminder that students need to encounter new words frequently in rich contexts:

1. Never seen the word before.

2. Knowing the word exists but not knowing what it means.

3. Having context-bound vague knowledge of the word's meaning.

4. Knowledge of a word but not being able to recall it readily enough to use it appropriately.

5. Knowing and being able to use a word appropriately.

(Beck, Mckeown & Omanson 1987)

Vocabulary and Reading Comprehension

Context and definition

Two sources of information are used to establish word meanings: context and definition. Both are important for building vocabularies.

Context refers to the text around the word that influences the definition, or sometimes even defines it. 'In-text' definitions are usually reserved for technical vocabulary present in non-fiction texts, and occasionally for when the narrator in classic children's literature intervenes to explain a word or phrase to a novice reader, usually in a patronising tone. The intrusive narrator is less familiar in contemporary children's literature, except in parodies such as Lemony Snicket's *Series of Unfortunate Events*:

'The phrase "in the dark," as I'm sure you know, can refer not only to one's shadowy surroundings, but also to the shadowy secrets of which one might be unaware.'

Definitional meanings are located in dictionaries.

Historically, school age students have been taught to use dictionaries to look up word meanings but, from our observations, instruction on the effective use of context alongside dictionary definitions is less evident in practice.

Pause for thought

Write a dictionary definition for the word 'mirror'.

When you have done this compare your answer with one of the definitions below. How similar or different were they?

Mirror:

1 polished or smooth surface (e.g. of polished metal or silvered glass) that forms images by reflection.

2 something that gives a true representation

Longman Dictionary of the English Language

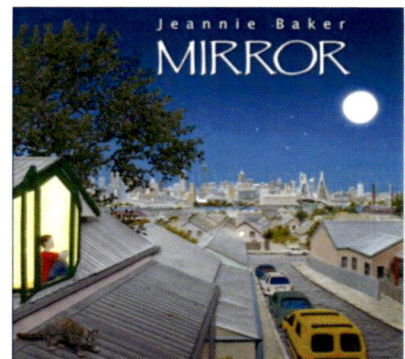

Walker Books

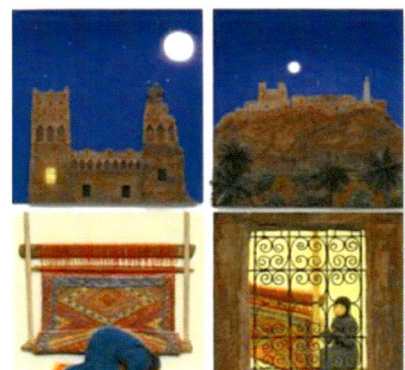

Walker Books

Was your definition similar to one of these dictionary definitions, or did you have something different? The contexts in which the word 'mirror' might be used are very rich and diverse. Perhaps you wrote a definition for 'to mirror' - mimicking or imitating? Or you may have defined it as a description of a synchronized routine in gymnastics or dance. In the poem *The Lady of Shalott*, the mirror is used as a symbol of isolation. The Lady can only view shadows of the real world in her mirror; it separates her from a normal existence. In *Snow White*, the mirror is a window to the soul of the wicked queen. The symbolic meanings of 'mirror' are not covered by the dictionary definitions above.

The wordless picture book *Mirror* by Jeannie Baker tells two stories simultaneously. One is the day in the life of a boy and his family living in a Middle Eastern country, the other the story of a boy and his family living in Australia. One family makes carpets, the other goes shopping for a new carpet for their home. In spite of the book's title, there are no mirrors in the story, only an ever-present moon, which both boys see at night.

A dictionary definition of the word 'mirror' will be insufficient for explaining precisely why Jeannie Baker has titled her book *Mirror*, through it might help refine an understanding, if accompanied by discussion and dialogue.

Vocabulary and Reading Comprehension

⏸ Pause for thought

Before reading the next section, take some time to reflect or discuss with other teachers:

- How do you currently teach vocabulary?

- How do you select words for vocabulary instruction?

- Do you categorise words for different types of vocabulary instruction?

- To what extent does vocabulary play a part in your selection of texts?

We assert that vocabulary teaching has been the *Cinderella* of literacy teaching in British schools. In the observation and fact gathering period of the 4XR project, we witnessed interesting work regarding the use of appropriate vocabulary at the point of writing in the project schools. Teaching frequently focussed on teaching parts of speech. Typical activities included generating adjectives, alternative verbs for 'said' or 'strong verbs'. We
found that teachers were keen to encourage an interest in words. 'Word of the week' walls were popular and featured words were often polysyllabic, high interest words. A typical example in a year 5 class was the word 'antidisestablishmentarianism.' There is no doubt that this appealed to the students, who relished learning these new 'difficult' words. Towards the end of the project we noticed that changes to the English curriculum brought about an increase in the instances of teaching morphological awareness and etymology as part of the spelling curriculum.

However, the teaching of vocabulary for reading comprehension was less evident and not as well articulated. In one of our workshops we outlined the research linking vocabulary instruction and reading comprehension and introduced some teaching strategies.

In this section we outline the rationale we used for selecting words to teach and the most successful teaching approaches that were used and refined by teachers in school.

Selecting words to teach

Although it is impossible to arrive at an exact number of words in the English language, the Oxford English Dictionary includes close to 250,000 words, excluding inflections, technical vocabulary and regional words. When these are taken into account it is estimated that the figure approaches 750,000 words. Clearly it would be impossible to provide instruction for all new vocabulary. Therefore it is important that teachers know which words to teach and the most productive ways of teaching them in order to ensure that students acquire robust vocabularies.

Beck et al (2002) offer a helpful approach to classifying vocabulary, which is designed to help teachers make these choices.

Tier Three words: low frequency, specialised words that may appear in specific fields or content areas (such as science or social studies).

Tier Two words: frequently occuring words that are central to comprehension, and are understood by most language users (without language delays). These words are great for explicit, targeted instruction.

Tier One words: basic words that appear in most students' vocabulary (without language delays).

Beck, McKeown & Kucan (2002)

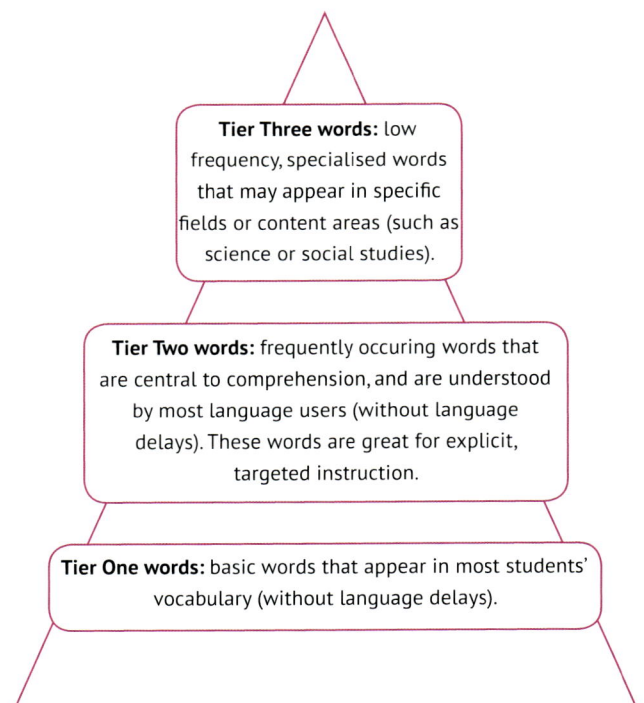

Vocabulary and Reading Comprehension

The significance of this classification is that it introduces the notion of usefulness. Selecting words for deep language instruction takes into account the utility of the words, not only the lack of familiarity, the complexity or the WOW! factor associated with using polysyllabic words. Thus a focus on teaching tier two words was a focus for development in project schools.

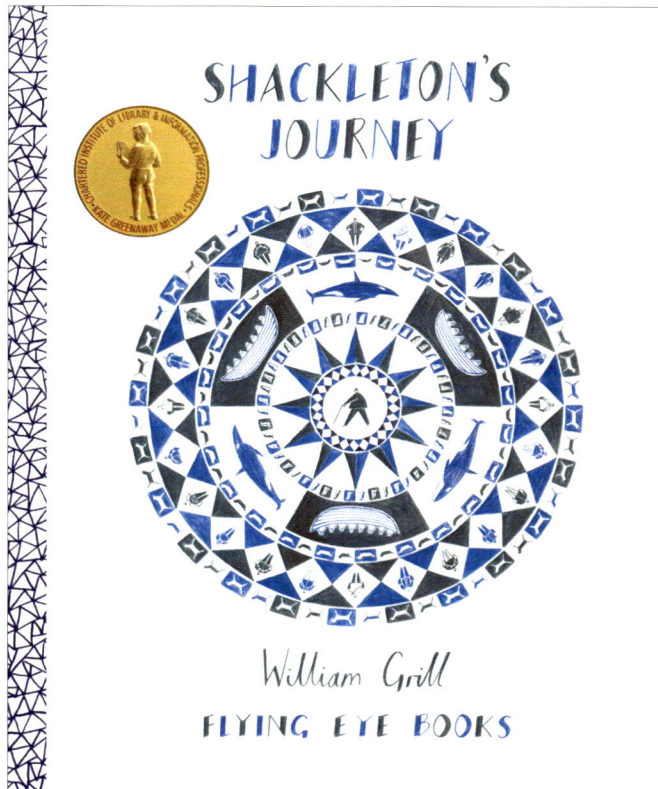

Flying Eye Books

STRATEGIES

Top tips for selecting tier two words

• Students may already have a way of expressing a concept for a tier two word. So learning these words gives them opportunities to be increasingly specific in their word choices.

• Some words are central to understanding the text.

• Many words in English are polysemic. Students may misinterpret texts if they know one meaning but are not conversant with alternative meanings.

• Words that are apparently simple may be conceptually complex. Understanding at the surface level may inhibit comprehension when the word is used in a slightly different context.

Vocabulary and Reading Comprehension

Selecting words from a class novel or text: an example

This extract is taken from the beginning of chapter one of Sonya Hartnett's *Children of the King*.

The words in the left hand column highlighted in yellow have been identified by the teacher as potential target words for vocabulary instruction. In the right-hand column the teacher has provided a commentary and a teaching decision.

The detail given in this example is not intended as a model that needs to be followed, rather it is to exemplify the kinds of thinking that take place in relation to selecting words. Most of this thinking is done as the teacher reads the text in advance for preparation. Typically five to seven words are selected in an average length chapter from a novel suitable for reading with nine to eleven year olds.

She heard it: footsteps in the dark. Cecily Lockwood, aged recently twelve **quailed** in the darkness beneath her bed and listened to the steps coming closer.	**Vocabulary commentary:** The word 'quailed' is unlikely to be familiar to most students. However, the general mood and tone can be understood from the context without knowing precisely what this word means. It is a tier two word but it has limited use and is more usual in older texts. **Teaching decision:** Give a definition for 'quailed' during reading.
The curtains of her bedroom were **drawn** and only a **ribbon** of light **nosed** past the door, and sense told Cecily that she must be nearly invisible in the blackness: but she did not feel invisible. Her teeth bit her lip.	**Vocabulary commentary:** 'Drawn' has more than one meaning but it is likely that most students will know the verb to draw the curtains. It can also mean: pale and haggard; to pull something out of a pocket e.g. to draw a pistol; to sketch or make an image or to shrink. Drawn is a good tier two word. 'Ribbon' may be familiar as a strip of material for tying hair but is less likely to be known in a more generalised context e.g. a long narrow strip (as in vegetables cut into ribbons) or metaphorically as a ribbon of light. Ribbon is a good tier two word. While students will know the noun 'nose' the use of 'nosed' in this context is more likely to be found in literary texts and may be confusing to some readers. **Teaching decision:** There is no need to take any action with the word 'ribbon'. 'Drawn' or 'nosed' could be selected as words to teach after reading.
Her heart bounced like a **trout**.	**Vocabulary commentary:** Some students will not know what a trout is. It's not essential to the meaning of the text. **Teaching decision:** Give an incidental definition. Briefly explain that a trout is a type of fish. The simile could be explored in a discussion about the effect of specific language features.

Vocabulary and Reading Comprehension

The footsteps had climbed the stairs. Cecily had heard the creak of each tread.	**Vocabulary commentary:** 'Creak' will probably be understood by most students in context. Other uses for the word such as 'creaking at the seams' may not be familiar. It is a good tier two word.
	'Tread' has more than one meaning. The verb 'to tread' is probably known by most students. The noun 'tread' meaning the top surface of a step or stair is unlikely to be known. Tread is a good tier two word.
	Teaching Decision: 'Creak' or 'tread' could be selected as word to teach after reading.
The steps had come stealthily along the hall, pausing in each doorway.	**Vocabulary commentary:** 'Stealthily' is likely to be known by some but not all of the students. Stealth may for instance be familiar, as with the word 'stealth' used to describe an ability in some computer games. They are unlikely to know phrases such as 'stealth tax'. Stealth and stealthily are words that are used in many different contexts and so 'stealthily' is a good tier two word.
	Teaching decision: 'Stealthily' could be selected to teach after reading.
Cecily pictured Jeremy folded under his bed, his heart flipping and diving. But no; Jeremy was too smart to hide under a bed. Jeremy would hide somewhere that could keep him secret all night. Only Cecily was silly enough to hide under a bed.	**Vocabulary commentary:** 'Folded' is a word in common usage and will be familiar to the students in different contexts. They may not have encountered the word used as it is here. Other uses of fold include the noun 'a fold' in a bedsheet or cloth or as a verb to fold or wrap something in cloth. Fold is a good tier two word.
	'Flip' and 'flipping' have many different uses. The literary use of flipping here is unlikely to be familiar, though the students may understand this usage in relation to flipping or turning over a coin. From which 'flip-side' is also derived. The word is also used as a mild expletive, and in financial markets to flip means to sell. Flip is a good tier two word.
	'Diving' is most commonly associated with making a dive into water, which can be an athletic dive or submerging into water as with a submarine. It is also used more generally to signal a sharp drop or fall as in shares in the stock market taking a dive. Unrelated uses include slang references to a disreputable club or taking a deliberate fall in boxing or football. In this instance Cecily is imagining Jeremy in a nervous, anticipatory state with his heart pounding irregularly 'flipping and diving'. Dive is a good tier two word.
	Teaching decision: fold, flip and dive are all candidates for teaching after reading.

Vocabulary and Reading Comprehension

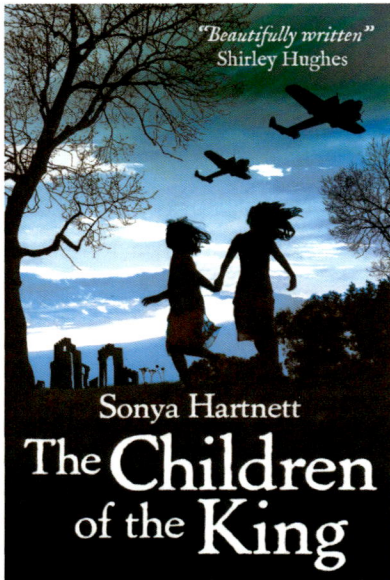

Scholastic

> **"**
>
> *This process tunes you in to selecting words to teach. I'm aware of making more informed decisions about vocabulary teaching now.* **"**
>
> *Year 5 teacher*

Selecting words from a class novel or text – as identified in *Children of the King*

Potential words to teach: drawn, nosed, creak, tread, stealth, fold, flip, dive.

Having made this assessment of potential teaching vocabulary, the teacher selected the best words for teaching. In making the final selection consideration was given to:

- making sure no two words have meanings that are too similar as this could lead to confusion

- including words that have the widest possible usage. In the selection above 'nosed' and 'tread' have a narrower range of definitions than the other words.

The teacher selected 'drawn' 'stealth' and 'dive' as target words for teaching. These words were added to the teacher's text potential diagram (see p13).

✏ Classroom activity

This activity is designed to help you think about selecting words for teaching and can be carried out individually, or used as a professional development activity for a staff meeting.

Select a passage of about 200 words from a novel, or text that you are reading with the class or a guided group.

- Highlight interesting vocabulary that you think has teaching potential.

- Insert the text into a two-column table as shown. In the left-hand column, paste the highlighted text. In the right-hand column, write your commentary on the highlighted words and your teaching decisions.

- Finally, from the list of possible words for teaching, select those which you consider to be most relevant and have the greatest potential for building a robust vocabulary.

⏸ Pause for thought

Before reading the next section, reflect or discuss with other teachers how you might adapt the approach to teaching vocabulary:

- before reading

- during reading

- after reading.

Vocabulary and Reading Comprehension

What are the best ways to teach vocabulary?

The National Reading Project (2000) reviewed more than 20,000 research citations and identified from the body of work 50 significant studies for detailed evaluation in order to determine how vocabulary can best be taught and related to reading comprehension processes. The following approaches are informed by current research.

First of all, it is useful to think about your goals for teaching vocabulary. There are two main purposes:

- clarification

- vocabulary enrichment.

Your intention will determine how you plan to teach.

In 4XR project schools we found that there was some overlap between the two goals and that vocabulary enrichment was sometimes a necessary precursor to clarification. The following example illustrates how a group of year 4 children struggled with the poem *Maggie Dooley* by Charles Causley. The poem is a character sketch of an old woman who visits the park each day to feed a group of stray cats. It includes the lines;

Macmillan

She sits by the children's

Roundabout

And takes a sip

From a bottle of stout.

She smiles a smile

And nods her head

Until her little

Family's fed.

The word 'family', combined with the pronoun 'her' proved problematic as the students couldn't move beyond the notion that family must refer to Maggie's children, even though there is no other mention of children in the poem. However, a second group, received some vocabulary enrichment prior to reading the poem, which led to greater conceptual understanding. The second group created semantic maps (see p44) of the concept 'family' which included attributes such as security. Thus the pre-reading exploration of the key word 'family' was used to create a bridge to understanding which the students brought into play when they subsequently read the poem.

It is interesting that when we have asked teachers to identify words that they think will be inhibit understanding of the poem the 'bottle of stout' is usually picked out. The best approach in this instance is to offer a quick definition as students don't need lengthy explanations in order to comprehend the poem.

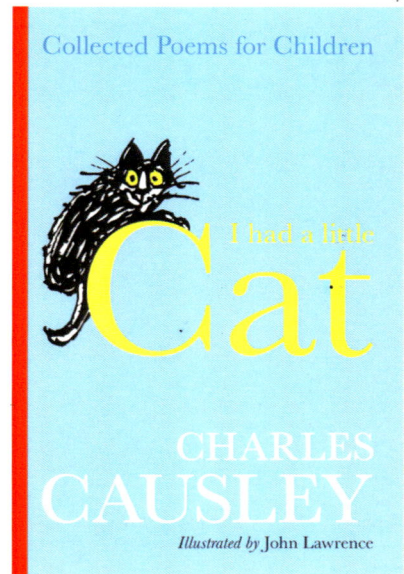

> **"**
> *I was surprised that an apparently simple word like 'family' could prevent the children from understanding the poem.*
> **"**
>
> *Judy Corry, Sheen Mount Primary school*

43

Vocabulary and Reading Comprehension

Clarification

Some words will need clarification in order for students to be able to understand a text. These will often be technical.

Generally, clarification of vocabulary is best dealt with during reading, especially if this is in the context of reading aloud to the class, group or one to one reading. In the previous used extract from *The Children of the King*, the teacher decided to simply clarify the words 'quailed', 'trout' and 'nosed'. Explanations that are given parenthetically should be quick and to-the-point so the flow of reading isn't disrupted.

In some cases, it might be useful to clarify words that are likely to interfere with comprehension, *prior* to reading. This is best reserved for tasks when students are asked to read extracts or short episodes independently.

It may also be helpful to give some guidance prior to reading on words that are likely to be difficult to pronounce. Sometimes hearing the word pronounced by the teacher before encountering them in the text will avoid confounding the reader.

Sometimes a word will be clarified within the text and students' attention can be drawn to how this is done, either with **emboldened** text and a glossary or the use of parenthetic commas. It is most usual to find these devices in non-fiction texts, although some educational publications might also include them in fiction texts.

Vocabulary enrichment

Over 70% of English words are polysemic. This makes English a rich and complex language in which meanings are often finely nuanced.

Multiple encounters with words are needed in order for them to impact on students' comprehension. Once words have been selected for teaching they should be revisited in varied ways with opportunities for students to make connections between words.

Semantic mapping

This graphic strategy establishes the schematic relationship between words and enables students to develop a deeper understanding of concepts, such as family, love, window, wild, mirror etc. In the 'Maggie Dooley' example quoted in this chapter, a narrow concept of family prevented students from understanding the poem.

Through semantic mapping, students activate and organise their prior knowledge. They are guided to structure their knowledge into formal relationships. And through reading and revisiting their maps they elaborate and refine their understanding.

All concepts have at least three different types of association:

- association of class – the order of things. So within the class family we might include mother, father, brother, sister etc

- association of property – these are the attributes that define the concept so for family these might include home, security, belonging

- associations of example – the Royal family, my family, a pride of lions.

Semantic maps are created by the teacher and students together through dialogue, making explicit the different types of association between groups of words.

Vocabulary and Reading Comprehension

Working with semantic maps: an example

In the 4XR project schools we have seen many instances of semantic mapping being used to develop a layered understanding of key words. In the example below a class of year 6 students has been reading Kevin Crossley-Holland's short story 'The Wild Man'.

Prior to reading the story the students had read *Beowulf* by Kevin Crossley-Holland, which presents a conventional portrait of the monster Grendel and paints a heroic image of the vanquisher, Beowulf.

'The Wild Man' is written from Grendel's point of view, although he isn't named in the text.

- After the reading the teacher highlights the word 'wild' in the title and gives the students two minutes to write a list of all the words they associate with the target word.

- After two minutes the teacher gathers the students and invites them to suggest words which she adds to the IWB without comment. Where the link between the suggested words and the target word are not clear, she asks the student to provide a justification for suggesting the word. Providing the explanation is valid then the word is added to the list.

STRATEGIES

Words suggested by the students:

animals	fierce	savage	feral	uninhabited	rough	storm
forest	desert	beast	plants	'out of control'	fierce	violent
nature	deserted	overgrown	uncontrolled	aggressive	attack	howling
mad	frantic	natural	nature	desolate	weather	werewolf

- during the collection of words the teacher made a couple of suggestions designed to encourage the students to think more broadly. The word 'civilised' was followed by several antonyms suggested by the students including 'tame'

- the teacher reviewed the list with the students and invited them to suggest links between words. One suggestion was that some words referred to wild places. These included 'uninhabited', 'forest' 'desert' Another suggestion was that some words referred to behaviour: 'fierce', 'mad', 'frantic', 'rough', 'aggressive', 'violent', 'attack' etc

- the teacher modelled how to group these words. She explained that a word could fit in more than one group

- the students worked in small groups to complete their semantic maps and then fed back to the class.

Vocabulary and Reading Comprehension

"

After we had listed our words we wrote them on post-its and moved them around to make one large semantic map, which we displayed in the classroom.

"

Year 5 teacher

Working with semantic maps: an example (continued)

- The teacher prompted the students to reflect and asked them to discuss in pairs:

  - What meanings of the word 'wild' are implied by the title 'The Wild Man'?

  - Who is the 'wild man'?

  - What evidence can you find to support your ideas?

- The subsequent discussion demonstrated some important shifts in thinking. 'Wild' was no longer seen as a wholly negative quality. The students highlighted evidence that suggested the use of 'wild' suggested natural rather than aggressive: *'My friends are seals. They dive as I do, and swim as I do. Their hair is like my hair. I sing songs with their little ones.'* One student suggested that the behaviour of the men in the story could be considered 'wild' . *'They fell on me then and twisted my arms, and hurt me.'*

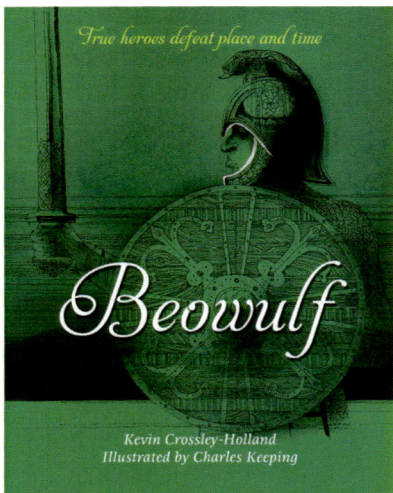

OUP

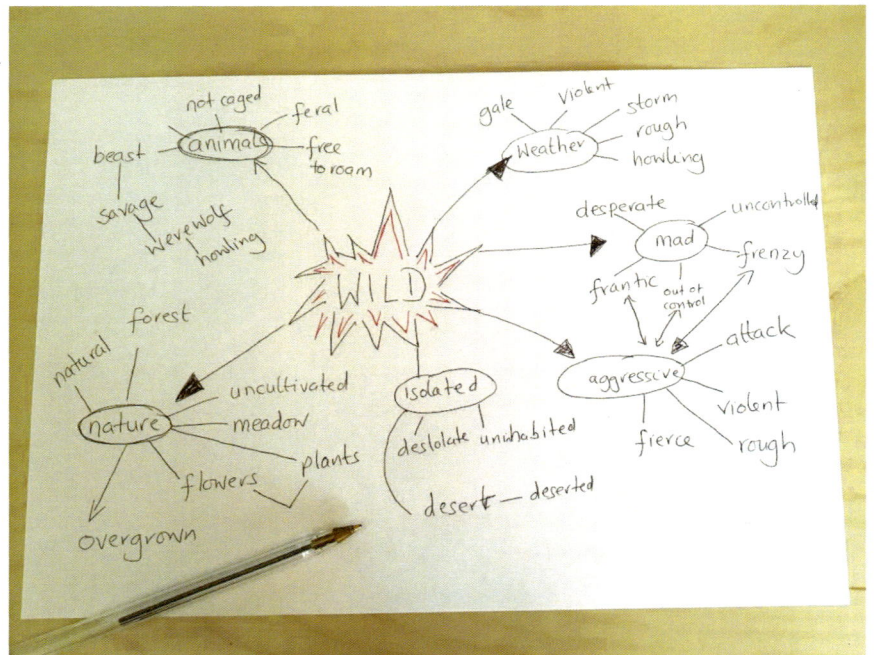

 Top tip

Lexipedia www.lexipedia.com is a free tool which generates semantic maps. It shouldn't be used to replace the process described above as the rich dialogue is essential for concept building. However, it is a useful supplementary tool and students might be interested to compare their own maps with those generated by the Lexipedia software, for identifying any aspects of the word that they have omitted. Lexipedia also categorises words into different parts of speech and provides dictionary definitions.

Vocabulary and Reading Comprehension

Vocabulary journals

A good vocabulary journal is essential for supporting vocabulary development. Unlike personal dictionaries which usually have two columns, one for new words and one for definitions, a vocabulary journal is *process led*. Students are introduced to new words, which are discussed and recorded in the students' journal prior to looking up definitions in the dictionary and analysing them.

Beck, McKeown and Kucan suggest the following six row format which we introduced to project schools, using the following process:

- after reading a text the target words are selected

- the students locate the target word in the text and write the sentence in the second row

- working in pairs or small groups the students discuss any clues to the meaning and also talk about any instances where they might have seen or heard the word. These are shared with the class

- following discussion, the words are looked up in dictionaries, with more than one definition being used for comparison. The definitions are discussed in relation to the way the word is used in the text

- word spies: students are encouraged to look for further instances of word use for homework and record them in their vocabulary journals

- these are shared at the end of the week.

> **"**
> *I combine the use of vocabulary journals with visual word walls. The students collect images depicting the target word and these are displayed and added to over the week.*
> **"**
>
> *Year 3 teacher*

STRATEGIES

Target word	Declaration
How is it used in the text?	"Mr Oakley, with the declaration of war imminent ..."
What clues to the words meaning can you see?	declare (to say something) -ation (the action or process of doing something)
Examples of where you have heard or seen the word	I think I have heard it at a wedding; "I now **declare you man and wife**." When a cricket team declares it means they finish the innings even if they haven't played all ten wickets
Dictionary definitions (more than one dictionary)	a positive, explicit, or formal statement proclamation: a declaration of war.
New examples / quotations	'Tis the voice of the Lobster I heard him declare. You have baked me too brown, I must sugar my hair.'

Pinterest

Pinterest is a useful support for building contextual knowledge. Students collect visual images and post them to Pinterest boards. An example of a Pinterest board for the target word 'declaration' could include a picture of Thomas Jefferson's 'Declaration of Independence' a photograph of Malcolm X with the quotation 'I do declare we shall overcome', a declaration of love and a face cream called 'Declare'. It is important that the Pinterest board is used to facilitate a discussion about the connections between the images and not used solely as a decorative collection of pictures.

Vocabulary and Reading Comprehension

Puffin Books

Top tip

A digital tool which can be used to support dictionary work, when combined with the process described above, is the website Lingro **www.lingro.com**. Type in the URL of any website and every word on the page becomes immediately hyperlinked to a dictionary definition. A word of caution here: it is important not to be seduced by the wizardry but always bear in mind the purpose for using the tool.

Dictionaries and vocabulary development

Dictionaries are not solely used as a source for word definitions; they contain a lot of useful information about word usage, derivations, pronunciation and etymology. But how useful are dictionaries for building vocabulary? Using a dictionary to look up definitions for lists of hitherto unknown words is of limited benefit. However, dictionaries *are useful* as a source for clarifying the meaning of *known* words. Students will gain most benefit from dictionary work when the process is modelled as in the example below, taken from a year 6 class reading *Goodnight Mister Tom* by Michelle Magorian, using a think-aloud strategy.

Target word: Declaration

1. The teacher reads the text.

"Ah thank you, Mr Oakley," she paused and took a deep breath. "Mr Oakley, with the declaration of war imminent ..."

2. The students look up the definitions for 'declaration' in class dictionaries.

3. In the first instance one dictionary might be used, but as students gain confidence in using dictionaries, comparing definitions from different sources affords a discussion about subtle differences. For instance, a combination of the definitions below using 'official', 'announce' and 'formal' helps refine a definition that works for the context:

Merriam-Webster online dictionary	the act of making an official statement about something
Oxford Concise dictionary	Make known, announce openly
Longman Dictionary of the English Language	Make known formally or officially

4. The teacher thinks aloud: 'Hmm, it sounds as though something is about to be announced. I can see how that fits with these definitions. The Oxford Dictionary specifically uses the word announce which matches the context well and is more precise than 'making known'. The important thing in the story is that this is a declaration of war, which sounds very formal or official. So a precise definition for declaration which fits with this passage is 'a formal, official announcement.'

Vocabulary and Reading Comprehension

Morphological strategies

Morphology, the study of word structure including roots, suffixes and prefixes, is a powerful way to build vocabulary. A morpheme is the smallest unit of a word that has a meaning attached to it. Morphemes are either root words or affixes (suffixes and prefixes).

If students know what the morphemes mean, they are more able to use clues to decipher new words. Morphological awareness is an area that needs further research to determine the most effective strategies to support reading comprehension.

✏️ Classroom activity

Here's an example of one activity that we found generated worthwhile group discussion and encouraged word analysis.

- Make a collection of word cards.

- Each set of words shares either a root word, prefix or suffix.

- Distribute the cards, one to each student. Have them circulate the room looking for students with cards that belong to the same set.

- When the groups have assembled, ask the students to work out what the root or affix means before checking in a dictionary.

- Finally, ask the students to generate some new words using their root or affix and provide definitions e.g telepet: pet that you look after virtually. You are sent updates on your pet's health and occasional photographs.

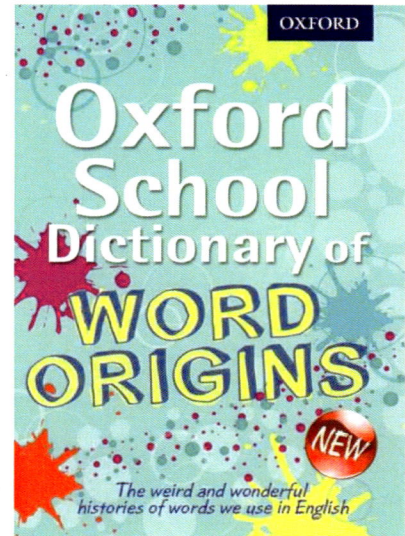

Oxford

> **"** *For effective vocabulary teaching a range of dictionaries is essential for discussing nuances in definitions.* **"**

duration	circle	telephone	transfer
endurance	circus	television	transport
durable	circumference	teleport	translate
	circumnavigate	telepathy	transmit
	circle		transect

Vocabulary and Reading Comprehension

Top ten wordsmiths

Read novels by these authors to enrich students' language:

Berlie Doherty

Marcus Sedgwick

Kevin Crossley-Holland

Frank Cottrell Boyce

Sonya Hartnett

Kate di Camillo

S F Said

Sally Gardner

David Almond

Lissa Evans

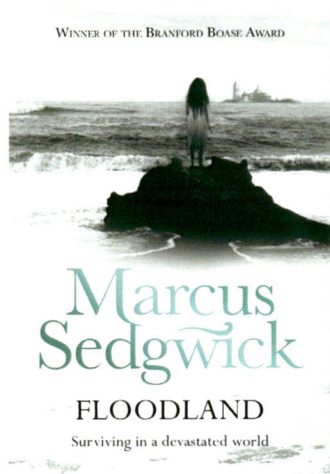

Orion Books

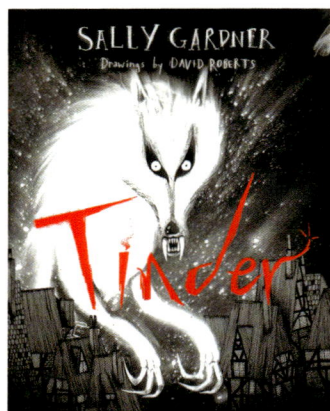

Orion Books

Read aloud

There is a significant difference between the words used in everyday language and written language. To quantify this we can count the number of instances of non-frequent word use, i.e. words not included in the 10,000 most frequently occurring words in spoken and written texts.

Adult spoken language	**17 words**
Children's novel	**30 words**
Adult novel	**52 words**

It is not surprising therefore that the amount of reading students do is very important to long term vocabulary development (Cunningham and Stanovich, 1998).

One of the problems identified by researchers is that students with higher initial vocabularies continue to learn more words from reading. However, the knowledge gap between students with high and initial vocabularies continues to widen. The exception is that when stories are read aloud to them, lower attaining students in particular benefit from the oral introduction of new vocabulary. This is especially true when coupled with discussion about the meaning of new words (Elley 1989).

As we noted in the chapter Selecting Texts, choosing texts which are well written and use language in interesting ways, to say interesting things, is important.

Pause for thought

This activity can be used to review provision in your class, or to plan a staff meeting focussing on the quality and range of class novels.

- Review the novels that are read aloud to students across the year.

- What do they offer in terms of range and quality of language?

- Do they introduce new and challenging vocabulary?

Vocabulary and Reading Comprehension

Further Reading

Beck, I.L., McKeown, M.G. & Kucan, L (2002) *Bringing Words to Life* New York: Guilford Press

Beck, I. L, McKeown, G. & Kucan, L. (2008) *Creating Robust Vocabulary* New York: Guilford Press

Butler, S. et al (2010) *A Review of the Current research of Vocabulary Instruction* National Reading Technical Assistance Center

Cain, K., & Oakhill,J. (2014). *Reading comprehension and vocabulary: Is vocabulary more important for some aspects of comprehension?* L'Année'Psychologique,' 114, 647-662.

Elfrieda H. Hiebert & Michael L. Kamil (Eds.) (2005) *Teaching and Learning Vocabulary: Bringing Research to Practice.* Mahwah, New Jersey: Lawrence Erlbaum Associates.

Elley, W. B. (1989). *Vocabulary acquisition from listening to stories.* Reading Research Quarterly, 24, 174—187.

Oulette, G (2006) *What's Meaning Got to Do With it: The role of Vocabulary in Word Reading and Reading Comprehension in* Journal of Educational Psychology 98,3: 554 - 566

Paris, S.G. & Stahl, S.A. (2005) *Children's Reading Comprehension and Assessment* Taylor & Francis

Proctor, C.P., Silverman, Harring, J., & Montecillo, C. (2012) *The role of vocabulary depth in predicting reading comprehension among English monolingual and Spanish-English bilingual children in elementary school in* Reading and Writing 25, 7: pp1635 – 1664

Ruddell, M. R. (1994). *Vocabulary knowledge and comprehension: A comprehension process view of complex literacy relationships.* In R. B. Ruddell, M. R. Ruddell, & H. Singer (Eds.), Theoretical models and processes

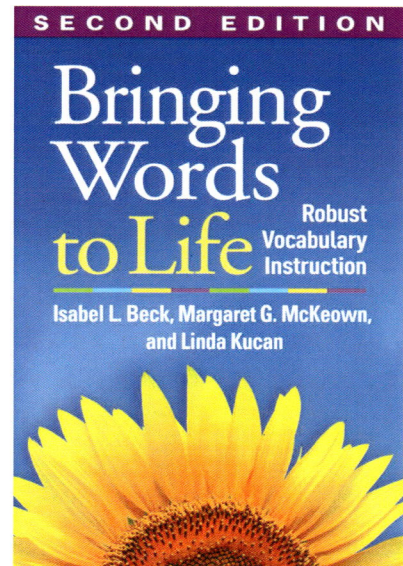

Guilford Press

Graphic Representation

Text structure and comprehension

Research across a range of disciplines including discourses analysis, cognitive psychology and rhetoric has asserted that knowledge of text structure has an impact on reading comprehension. The general consensus is that patterns in the organisation of text play important roles in how readers read. Yuill and Oakhill (1991) found that students with poor understanding of narrative structure are poor comprehenders of stories.

Why use graphic representation?

Graphic representations use linguistic and non-linguistic material to help students process material. They are useful for all students and may be especially useful for visual learners and those who find it difficult to process information that is presented in a linear format. Extensive research into the use of graphic organisers, especially those that expose text structure, indicates that they can be effective in leading students to analyse structure and identify patterns, which in consequence deepens reading comprehension (Jiang & Grabe, 2007). It should be noted that research findings do report differences in success rates and that the design of the organiser and instruction provided by the teacher is a significant element in determining success.

Before, during and after reading

Graphic representations have been used to develop reading comprehension since the 1980s. Informed by Schema Theory (Anderson 1977 and others) they were initially regarded as a valuable tool to activate prior knowledge, enabling students to relate new material to their existing experiences and understanding. They were often referred to as 'Advance Organisers' (Anderson and Pearson 1984).

More recent work highlights the potential to use graphic representation **during reading** to help guide the learner, and **after reading** to aid summarisation and make new learning explicit.

Introducing organisers

To ensure effective use, it is important to follow a process of modelling and guided practice in order that students are increasingly able to use the organisers independently. Ultimately they need to generate their own versions rather than memorising or copying the teachers' model, or filling in blank copymasters. Active engagement is essential (Manoli & Papdoupoulou 2012).

However, handing the process over to the students before it has been effectively modelled increases cognitive load as it forces students to grapple with new process tools as well as content learning. Thus, it is important that the transition is well-managed.

Teaching cycle

- **Modelling:** the students are shown a diagram or chart. The structure is explained and the teacher demonstrates how to complete it. At this stage the teacher checks that the students understand the purpose for using it and there are opportunities for questions.

- **Guided practice:** the students are guided through the steps needed to complete the tasks with verbal and visual instruction.

- **Independent use:** students have opportunities to use the diagram or chart independently

- **Innovation:** once established, students will be able to innovate and to add layers of sophistication. Some examples are given later in this section.

There are a great many visual and graphic organisers and variations but it is best to develop a portfolio of the most useful which are revisited regularly in order that they can be assimilated by the students. Once the basic organisers are understood, they can be adapted for more sophisticated use. The organisers outlined in this chapter are the ones that we have found most useful for supporting and developing reading comprehension both within English lessons and cross-curricular literacy.

Top tips for using graphic representation

- Students should draw their own organisers. Encourage them to develop their own versions once they have understood the basic structures.

- Allow the organisers to be used flexibly – students will need to add or take away boxes, to increase or decrease the number of connections, as appropriate.

- Vary the way the organisers are presented – make large versions for the classroom, use a variety of materials such as whiteboards and post-its.

- Embed the use of organisers in the learning and teaching cycle. Revisit and add to the maps at different stages in the teaching cycle.

- Use the organisers to generate high quality dialogue with students working in collaborative groups and whole class discussion.

- Demonstrate how the organisers can be used to develop summaries, structure writing, organise information that may be poorly structured.

- Don't expect students to sit in silence and fill boxes.

> *It is the talk that makes the learning experience powerful. Students learn to analyse, organise, synthesize and evaluate by talking in groups or in dialogue with the teacher.*

> *Organisers are not ends in themselves; they are a tool to support learning.*

> *Avoid using organisers as worksheets to keep students occupied as this will not result in deep learning.*

STRATEGIES

Graphic Representation

> **"**
>
> *Brainstorming ... allows students to engage with a topic, bring their own knowledge to bear and take risks with ideas ...*
>
> **"**

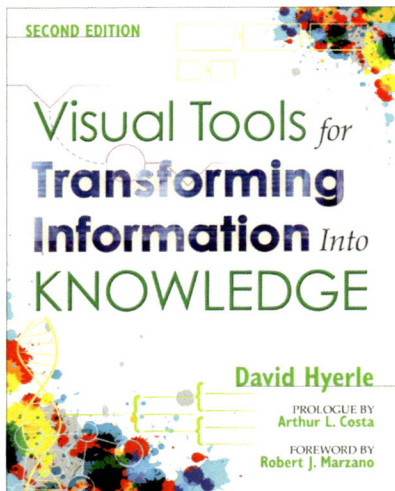

Corwin

Types of visual tool

Hyerle (2009) identifies four different types of visual tools:

- **brainstorming webs**

- **graphic organisers**

- **concept mapping**

- **thinking maps.**

There are similarities and cross-over between each of these categories and it can be distracting to get tied up in arguments about what a particular strategy is called. It is best to focus on how the tools you are using impact on students' reading comprehension. However, we have used Hyrle's categorisation to inform the organisation of this section as it allows us to highlight some of the similarities and differences.

Brainstorming webs

Why are brainstorming webs useful?

Brainstorming* is a technique used to encourage quick and creative thinking. As a group activity it allows ideas to be pooled and knowledge is constructed socially (Mercer 1995). It is an exploratory strategy which allows students to engage with a topic, bring their own knowledge to bear and take risks with ideas by avoiding self-editing too early in the process. This allows them to express both 'good' ideas, which might lead to fruitful avenues of enquiry, and 'bad' ideas, which may be discarded later. Allowing all ideas to be exposed provides an opportunity for critical thinking and group evaluation.

With regard to reading comprehension, brainstorming is most useful as a pre-reading strategy. It can be used to activate prior knowledge, make connections with new learning and track the acquisition of new knowledge across a sequence of work.

* The term 'brainstorming' rather than more recent alternative 'thought shower' is used here because it has been in use since the 1890s and Epilepsy Action state 'Our view is that it depends upon the context: if the word is being used to describe a meeting where participants are suggesting ideas, then its use is not offensive to people with epilepsy.'

How are they used?

There are several brainstorming techniques that can be used:

- listing all ideas on a given theme or subject

- clustering ideas (which can follow after listing)

- invisible writing (typing ideas with the computer screen turned off — discourages self-editing)

- questioning (notes are made in response to quick fire questions about who, what, where, why, how, when)

- observation (notes in response to sensory prompts e.g. what does it look like? what does it taste like? etc.)

- argument (notes about the pros and cons of an argument).

Typically students might be given a short time to make as many responses to a given question as possible. Questions should be open ended and might include:

- **what do you know** about fairy tales?

- **what ideas do you have** about what makes a good story?

- **are zoos a good thing?** List as many arguments for and against as possible.

This is followed by a collective sharing of ideas which are incorporated in the brainstorm map.

" … it can be used to activate prior knowledge, make connections with new learning and track the acquisition of new knowledge … "

STRATEGIES

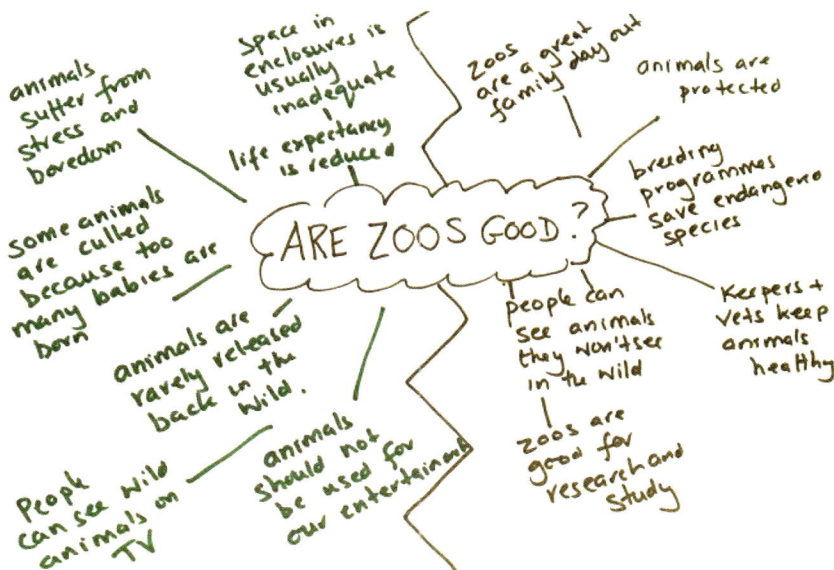

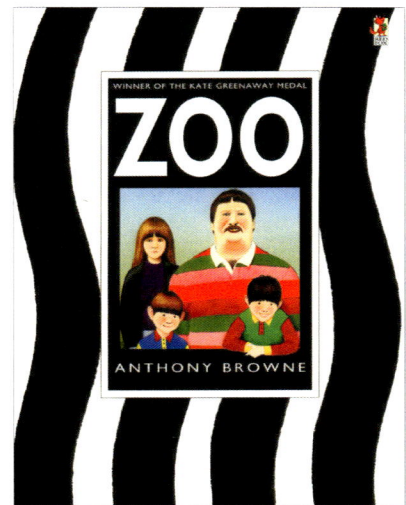

Red Fox

Graphic Representation

> *Instead of following step 5 of the Charette Procedure, I invited all the students in the class to move around and look at what the others had written on their whiteboards. After they had harvested ideas they returned to their home groups to discuss what they had learned.*

The Charette Procedure

The Charette Procedure is useful if you are conducting brainstorming sessions for students who are already familiar with brainstorming, and on occasions when you want to explore more than one facet of a topic.

1. Organise the class into small groups.

2. Each group is given a different aspect of the topic or a question to focus on.

3. Students are given a short period for individual brainstorming.

4. Each group selects a recorder to write down the group ideas.

5. Reporters visit each group to present their ideas – this step is repeated until the reporters have visited every group.

6. The groups revisit their ideas, incorporating and building on ideas from the other groups.

7. Finally the reporters feed back to the class.

Pause for thought

Think about a time when you have used brainstorming activities with your class.

- What are the merits and weaknesses of brainstorming?

- What needs to be considered to make brainstorming work well?

- Are there any changes you will make if you use this technique in the future?

Top tips for effective brainstorming

Effective brainstorming is contingent upon:

- Accepting students' ideas without criticism or judgement.

- Avoidance of teachers imposing their own ideas.

- Not privileging ideas that are present in a text.

- Not dismissing ideas that don't fit with the text.

- Sufficient opportunities for critical reflection and evaluation.

Graphic organisers

Graphic organisers are tools that are used to represent information graphically and are identified as one of the most effective evidence based teaching strategies (Petty, 2009).

Why are graphic organisers useful?

How do graphic organisers work? They:

- require the students to isolate and extract important information, enabling them to analyse relationships

- help students focus on text structure

- aid memory

- help students to summarise

- develop understanding of conceptual and content vocabulary

- create a record of learning, especially when the organisers are revisited, amended and added to through a learning sequence.

Types of graphic organiser used to support reading comprehension

Story maps

Story maps have been used in classrooms since in the 1980s (Beck and McKeown, 1981, Reutzel 1985) and they are familiar to most teachers. This technique helps students organise important elements of a story, thus developing knowledge and understanding of story grammar. Story maps extend students' existing story schema and improve comprehension when used in conjunction with interpretive, analytical and creative questions.

> **" **
>
> *When using graphic organisers make it explicit to students the connections between the type of organiser used and the type of thinking that it supports.*
>
> **"**

Pause for thought

Before reading this section, think about the following concepts. How would you represent them graphically?

- The relationship of the protagonist to all the other characters in a novel.

- The plots and sub-plot structure in a novel.

- The choices a character makes and the effect this has in a story.

- The similarities and differences between Hans Christian Andersen's *The Little Mermaid* and Oscar Wilde's *The Nightingale and the Rose*.

Top tips for using story maps

- Before reading – to activate prior knowledge e.g. construction of a story map for a well-known story.

- During reading – to guide through the text e.g. a blank story map completed during reading.

- After reading - to facilitate summarisation e.g. a completed story map used to help students write a story summary.

Graphic Representation

> "
>
> *We compared story maps for the Grimm's version of 'Little Red Cap' with Toby Forward's 'The Wolf's Story' and Bethan Woollvin's 'Little Red'. The story maps helped us reflect on different outcomes and concepts of justice, revenge, forgiveness, and prejudice in the stories.*
>
> "

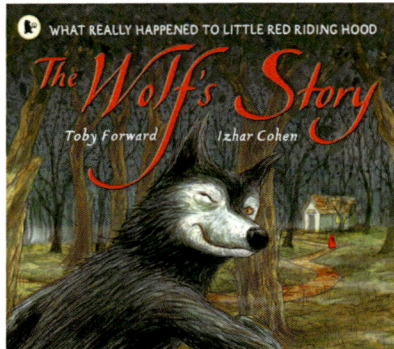

Walker Books

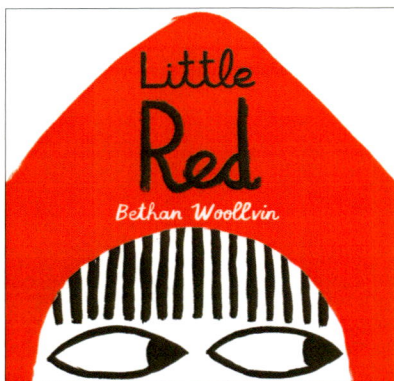

Macmillan (Two Hoots)

Story maps (continued)

Story maps can be constructed with the whole class in groups or individually and many teachers will have their favourite formats. The components of story maps are derived from the elements of a story:

- title (what is the story called?)

- characters (who are the major characters and the minor characters?)

- setting (where, when and over what period of time does the story take place?)

- plot (what is the problem, goal, motivation, action, key events, climax, resolution?)

- theme (what is the underlying meaning or moral of the story?).

! Example of a story map

In this example a year 4 class constructed a story map of a well-known folk tale before reading several alternative versions.

Title:	*'Little Red Cap' (based on the Brothers Grimm)*
Setting:	**Where:** *In a forest and grandma's cottage* **When:** *Long ago*
Characters:	*Little Red Cap, Big Bad Wolf, Grandma, The Woodcutter*
Problem:	*Delivering food to grandma without falling prey to the Big Bad Wolf*
Action:	**Event 1:** *Mother warns Little Red Cap to go direct to Grandma's house* **Event 2:** *Takes basket of goodies to Grandma but stops to talk to wolf* **Event 3:** *Takes the long path while wolf arrives at cottage and eats Grandma* **Event 4:** *Wolf dressed as Grandma attempts to fool Little Red Cap*
Outcome:	*Woodcutter arrives and saves the day*
Message:	*Do as your mother tells you and don't stop to talk to strangers in the forest.*

Story grammar questions?

Story maps are used to help students answer comprehension questions which draw attention to the way stories are structured:

- Where did this story take place?

- When did this story take place?

- Who were the main characters in this story?

- Were there any other important characters?

- What was the main problem in this story?

- How did ... try to overcome the problem?

- Was it hard to overcome the problem?

- Was s/he successful?

- Can you think of a different way that this story might have ended?

- What did you learn from reading this story?

What next?

Once students are confident at answering basic questions, the story maps can be developed to take account of more complex elements. For example, the section called 'Characters' might be expanded to include further details such as 'good characters' and 'bad characters' or 'protagonist' and 'antagonist'. The section called 'Action' might be further analysed by looking at the rising action (before the climax) climax (where the action is at its most intense) and the falling action (after the climax).

Questions become sophisticated, for example:

- Who is the hero in this story?

- Who is the anti-hero?

- What happens in the climax?

- How is the story resolved?

STRATEGIES

> *Story maps are useful while they continue to help students understand and analyse the structure of stories, but they can be discarded once the elements have been internalised.*

> *I had used story mapping before but now I am making more use of the maps. Rather than viewing them as an end product, I use them as active tools to scaffold and extend thinking.*
>
> *Year 4 teacher*

Graphic Representation

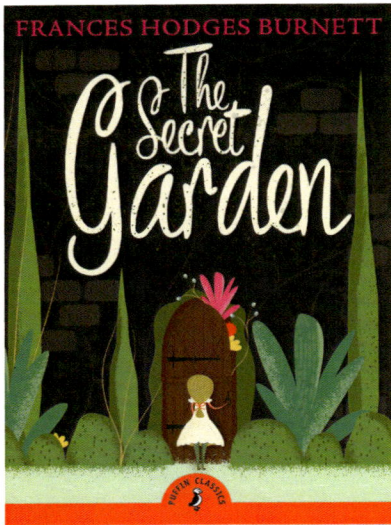

Puffin Classics

Theme Cards

In one year 6 class, the students were familiar with mapping the structure of a story but less experienced in identifying the themes. To enhance the use of story maps, we introduced theme cards as a means of promoting discussion about themes. The cards helped to equip students with language that enabled them to recognise and understand a greater range of themes in literature.

After reading the *The Secret Garden*, the students discussed the elements of the story and created a graphic organiser 'Finding a theme'

Finding a theme

Book title: *The Secret Garden*

Characters	Setting	Problem
Mary Dickon	A large manor house on the North Yorkshire Moors in the early part of the twentieth century	Mary Lennox is sent to live with her uncle and cousin. She is unhappy in her surroundings: • due to her own unpleasant character • her uncle and cousin's emotional problems

A lesson learned by a character
(review characters, problem, and summary)

Character name: Mary

Lesson learned: Mary learns that:

Nature is magical.

"And the secret garden bloomed and bloomed and every morning revealed new miracles."

If you are pleasant to others they will repay you with kindness.

At the beginning *"People never like me and I never like people,"* she thought.

After meeting Dickon: *"Oh, how she did love that queer, common boy!"*

Hard work is repaid with rewards

Physical activity is good for you.

"At that moment a very good thing was happening to her. Four good things had happened to her, in fact, since she came to Misselthwaite Manor. She had felt as if she had understood a robin and that he had understood her; she had run in the wind until her blood had grown warm; she had been healthily hungry for the first time in her life; and she had found out what it was to be sorry for someone."

Graphic Representation

After completing the first sections, the teacher organised the class in pairs and distributed a set of theme cards to each pair. The teacher clarified the meaning of any cards that were not readily understood.

Dealing with loss	Growing up	You need to lead a healthy life to have a healthy mind	Friendship and loyalty are more important than wealth
Being in touch with the natural world leads to happiness	Truth is always better than secrets and lies	Always be true to yourself	Treat others as you would like to be treated yourself
Bad deeds are punished and good deeds are rewarded	Nature is more powerful and important than technology	Take risks if you want to be successful	True friends stick with you through thick and thin

"

I have found that one of the challenges for students in my class is that they don't have the language to help them talk about themes. Since introducing theme cards I have noticed the language creeping in to our discussions about books more often.

"

Year 6 teacher

The students then worked in pairs to decide which themes were relevant to the story and to find the evidence to support their choices.

Themes in *The Secret Garden*	Events which support this
NATURE: Being in touch with the natural world leads to happiness	Gaining the robin's confidence and developing a relationship: 'She had felt as if she had understood a robin and that he had understood her' Playing outside in all weathers 'She had run in the wind until her blood had grown warm.' Watching the efforts of gardening turn into a miracle: "And the secret garden bloomed and bloomed and every morning revealed new miracles."
HEALTH: You need to lead a healthy life to have a healthy mind.	

Top tip for constructing theme cards

When constructing theme cards, include some that have slight differences in meaning as well as others that are clearly different. It is important to remember that the way students respond to thematic content is determined by experience; being able to justify ideas is more important than reaching a consensus or expecting all students to respond to the dominant themes in the same way.

Graphic Representation

" *A key skill for readers is to be able to identify the main ideas and then find supporting details …* "

Graphic organisers for non-fiction texts

Pause for thought

Before reading the next section consider how would you use graphic representation to help your students understand structures in texts dealing with the following topics:

- the relationship between a television advertisement and a magazine advertisement

- the possible causes of global warming and potential solutions

- the arguments for and against students under 11 having mobile phones in school

- the causes of an event such as the First World War.

Graphic organisers can be used to support understanding of the different types of structure in non-fiction texts. The most common are:

Description	Information about a topic
Sequence	Events and ideas are presented in numerical or chronological order
Cause and effect	When ideas, events and facts are presented as causes with relating outcomes or effects
Compare and contrast	Similarities and differences are presented between two or more topics or concepts
Problem and solution	A problem is presented followed by one or more solutions. This may also include an evaluation and suggested best solution
Question and answer	A question is posed and then followed by answers.

Top tip for graphic organisers for non-fiction texts

Although this section deals primarily with non-fiction or expository text, some of these elements are also present in fiction and so these organisers can be used with fiction and poetry, where appropriate. For instance, a narrative event (cause) may have a number of outcomes (effects).

Graphic Representation

Description

Many texts provide information about a topic, which can be through a variety of media. A key skill for readers is to be able to identify the main ideas and then find supporting details.

Examples of cue words and phrases for descriptive text	For instance, To illustrate, An example of..., To exemplify..., Such as..., For example..., Characteristically..., Typically, Key feature, Most noteworthy, A major event

STRATEGIES

Simple graphic organisers used to help students locate information about a subject include Bubble Maps and Tree Maps (see Thinking Maps p72). In the 4XR project schools, teachers used a combination of highlighting and graphic organisers to help students identify important and supporting information.

In one year 6 class, the teacher prepared a copy of *The Watercress Girl* by Henry Mayhew for each student.

- The text was read aloud and first responses were discussed.

- The teacher explained the difference between main ideas (details which are essential to understanding the text) and supporting ideas (which provide additional information).

- Using an enlarged text on the IWB the teacher modelled highlighting main ideas. The students made suggestions.

- The students read the text again independently then used a yellow highlighter to mark keywords, phrases and sentences.

- Highlighted sections were shared and discussed with the class.

- The enlarged copy was highlighted showing only the agreed key points.

- The teacher modelled finding supporting information to add details to the main idea. Supporting ideas were highlighted in pink.

- The students returned to the text and highlighted supporting information in pink.

- The teacher gathered the class and after a brief discussion about the supporting details showed the students how to complete the graphic organiser.

- Finally the teacher explained how the graphic organiser provided a summary of the text.

Extract from *The Watercress Girl* by Henry Mayhew from London Labour and London Poor (1861)

The ==little watercress girl== who gave me the following statement, ==although only eight years of age==, had entirely ==lost all childish ways==, and was, indeed, in thoughts and manner, a woman. There was something cruelly pathetic in hearing this infant, so young that her features had scarcely formed themselves, talking of the bitterest struggles of life, with the calm earnestness of one who had endured them all. I did not know how to talk with her. At first I treated her as a child, speaking on childish subjects; so that I might, by being familiar with her, remove all shyness, and get her to narrate her life freely.

==I asked her about her toys and her games== with her companions; but the look of amazement that answered me soon put an end to any attempt at fun on my part. I then talked to her ==about the parks==, and whether she ever went to them. "The parks!" she replied in wonder, "where are they?" I explained to her, telling her that they were large open places with green grass and tall trees, where beautiful carriages drove about, and people walked for pleasure, and children played.

Her eyes brightened up a little as I spoke; and she asked, half doubtingly, "Would they let such as me go there--just to look?" ==All her knowledge seemed to begin and end with watercresses==, and what they fetched. ==She knew no more of London than that part she had seen on her rounds==, and ==believed that no quarter of the town was handsomer or pleasanter than it was at Farringdon-market or at Clerkenwell==, where she lived. Her little face, pale and thin with privation, was wrinkled where the dimples ought to have been, and she would sigh frequently. ==When some hot dinner was offered to her, she would not touch it, because, if she eat too much, "it made her sick," she said;== "and ==she wasn't used to meat,== only on a Sunday."

The poor child, ==although the weather was severe, was dressed in a thin cotton gown==, with a ==threadbare shawl== wrapped round her shoulders. She wore no covering to her head, and the long rusty hair stood out in all directions. When she walked she shuffled along, for fear that the large carpet slippers that served her for shoes should slip off her feet.

See completed organiser over the page

Graphic Representation

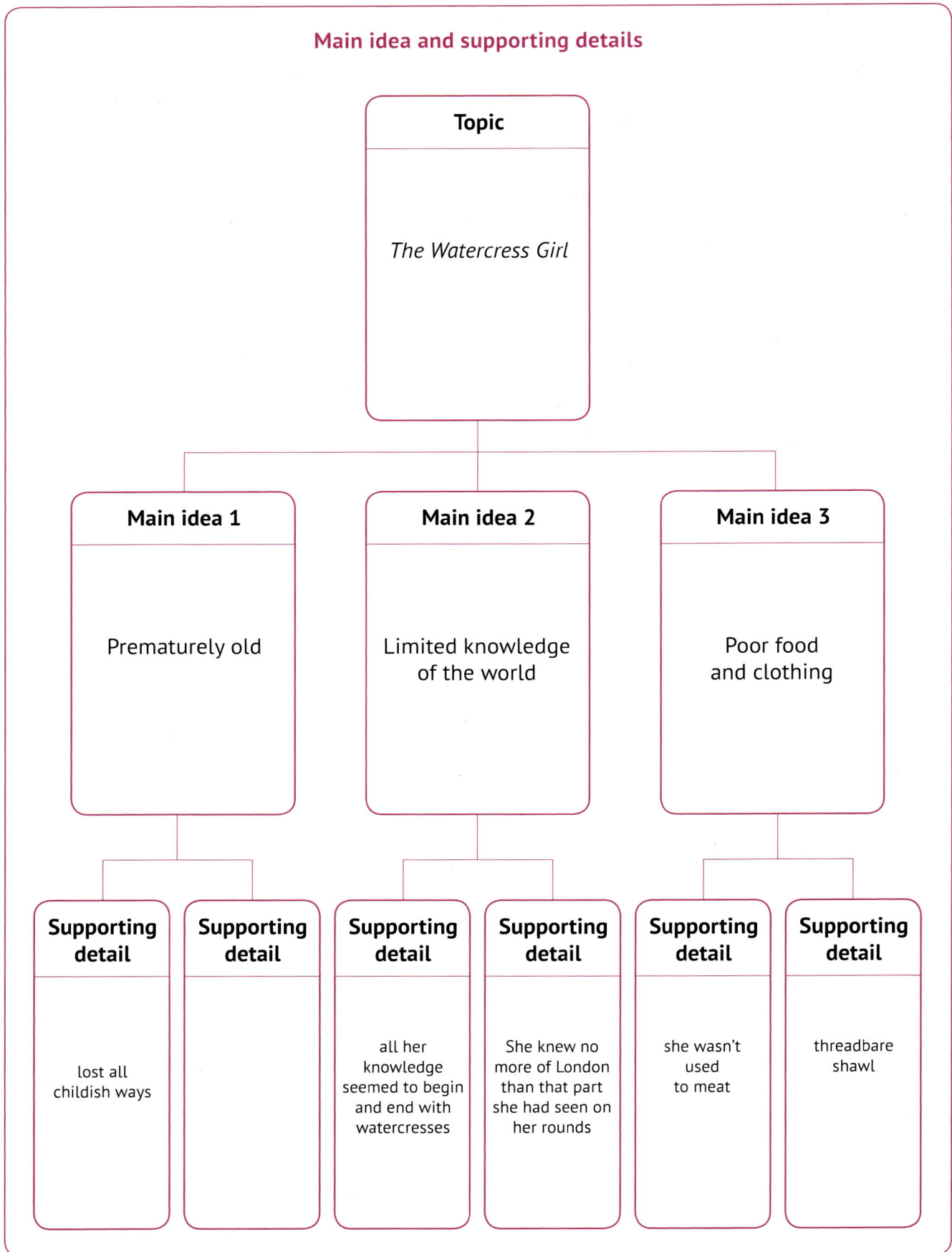

Main idea and supporting details

Topic
The Watercress Girl

Main idea 1	Main idea 2	Main idea 3
Prematurely old	Limited knowledge of the world	Poor food and clothing

Supporting detail	Supporting detail	Supporting detail	Supporting detail	Supporting detail	Supporting detail
lost all childish ways		all her knowledge seemed to begin and end with watercresses	She knew no more of London than that part she had seen on her rounds	she wasn't used to meat	threadbare shawl

Sequence and chronological text

Texts which explain a procedure process or recount events will include a sequence of ideas or events.

Examples of cue words or phrases for a sequence or chronological text	First, Second, Then, Earlier, Later, Soon, Before, After, Not long after, Initially, Finally, Much later, Following, I went next, So...

Simple organisers to help students with identifying a sequence include Story Boards and Flow Maps (see Thinking Maps p73)

An extract from Samuel Pepys Diary September 2, 1666

Some of our maids sitting up late last night to get things ready against our feast today, Jane called up about three in the morning, to tell us of a great fire they saw in the City. So I rose, and slipped on my night-gown and went to her window, and thought it to be on the back side of Mark Lane at the farthest; but, being unused to such fires as followed, I thought it far enough off, and so went to bed again, and to sleep. . . . By and by Jane comes and tells me that she hears that above 300 houses have been burned down tonight by the fire we saw, and that it is now burning down all Fish Street, by London Bridge. So I made myself ready presently, and walked to the Tower; and there got up upon one of the high places, . . .and there I did see the houses at the end of the bridge all on fire, and an infinite great fire on this and the other side . . . of the bridge. . . .

So down [I went], with my heart full of trouble, to the Lieutenant of the Tower, who tells me that it began this morning in the King's baker's house in Pudding Lane, and that it hath burned St. Magnus's Church and most part of Fish Street already. So I rode down to the waterside, . . . and there saw a lamentable fire. . . . Everybody endeavouring to remove their goods, and flinging into the river or bringing them into lighters that lay off; poor people staying in their houses as long as till the very fire touched them, and then running into boats, or clambering from one pair of stairs by the waterside to another. And among other things, the poor pigeons, I perceive, were loth to leave their houses, but hovered about the windows and balconies, till they some of them burned their wings and fell down.

Having stayed, and in an hour's time seen the fire rage every way, and nobody to my sight endeavouring to quench it, . . . I [went next] to Whitehall (with a gentleman with me, who desired to go off from the Tower to see the fire in my boat); and there up to the King's closet in the Chapel, where people came about me, and I did give them an account [that]dismayed them all, and the word was carried into the King. so I was called for, and did tell the King and Duke of York what I saw; and that unless His Majesty did command houses to be pulled down, nothing could stop the fire. They seemed much troubled, and the King commanded me to go to my Lord Mayor from him, and command him to spare no houses.

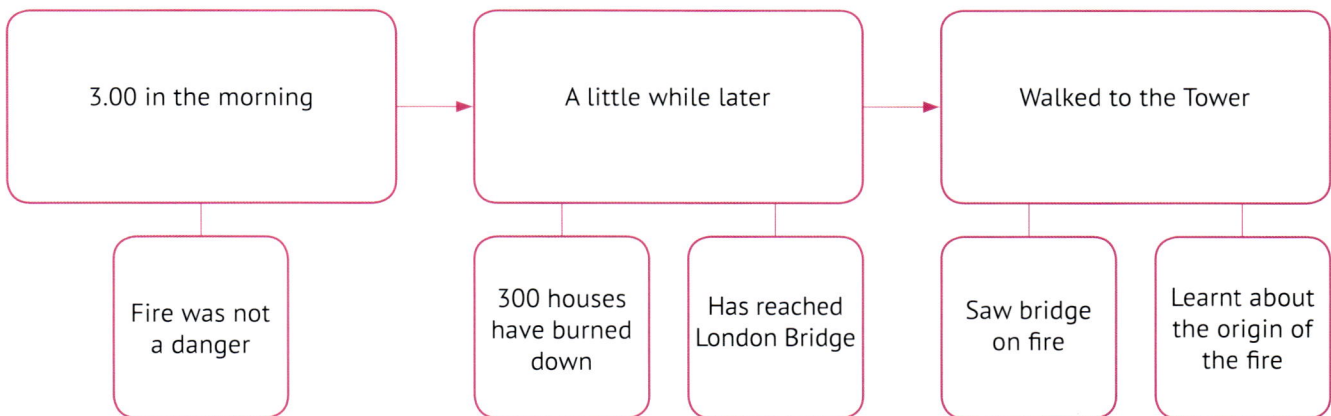

3.00 in the morning	A little while later	Walked to the Tower
Fire was not a danger	300 houses have burned down / Has reached London Bridge	Saw bridge on fire / Learnt about the origin of the fire

Top tip for sequence and chronological text

Storyboards are well used in primary classrooms particularly with fictional texts, but can also be used to show sequence in expository text.

Graphic Representation

Cause and effect

Cause and effect (where ideas, events and facts are presented as causes with relating outcomes) may be used when writing about history, science experiments, geographical processes and narrative events, among others.

Example cue words and phrases for a cause and effect text	Accordingly, Consequently, May be due to, As a result of, If.... Then..., Therefore, May be due to

A single cause may have multiple effects or conversely, a number of factors might result in a single effect. Graphic organisers such as Multi-flow diagrams (see Thinking Maps p74) can be used to help students understand the structure of cause and effect writing. Students will need to be taught to identify which type of organiser is relevant to their current reading:

• one cause with multiple effects

• many causes and many effects

• many causes with one effect.

In the example shown below, a class of year 6 students had been studying the causes of the First World War using several texts and web based sources.

Multi-flow Map

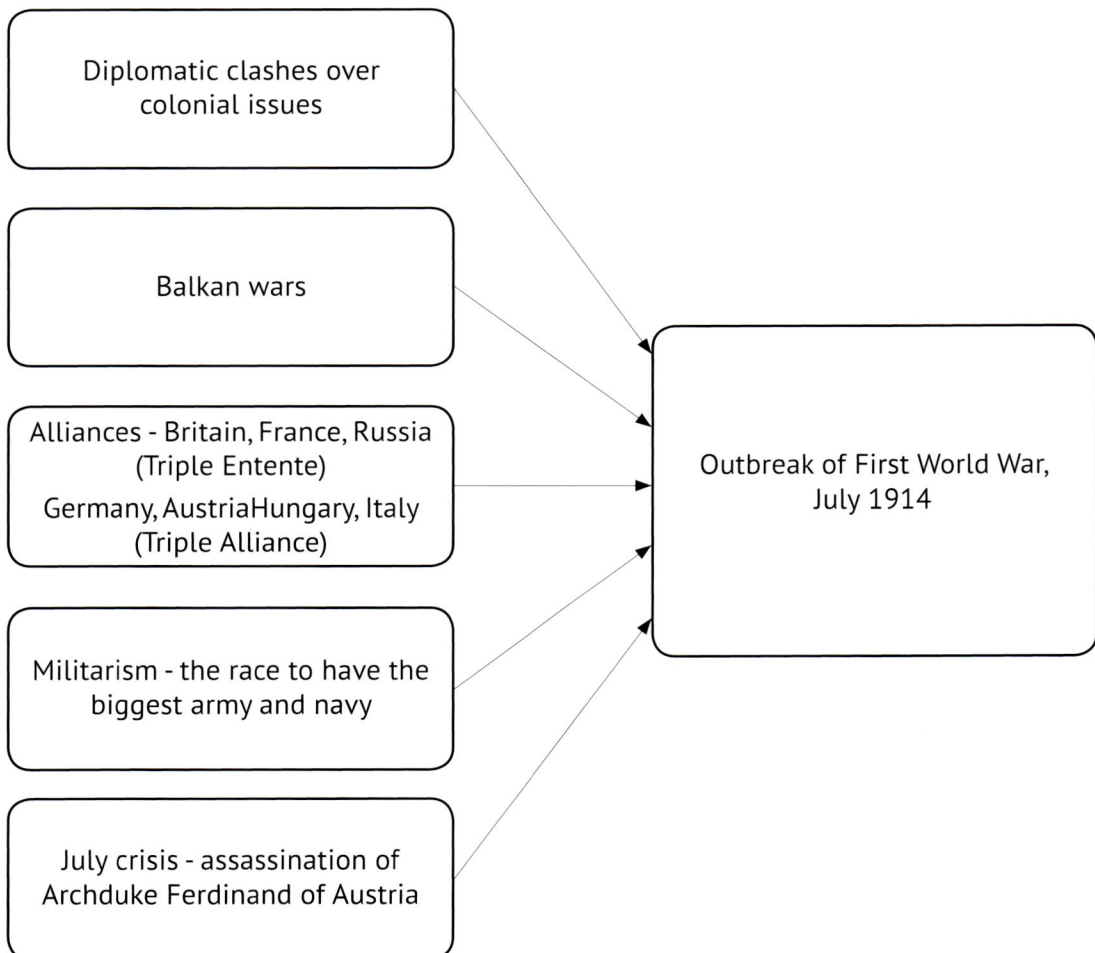

Diplomatic clashes over colonial issues

Balkan wars

Alliances - Britain, France, Russia (Triple Entente) Germany, AustriaHungary, Italy (Triple Alliance)

Militarism - the race to have the biggest army and navy

July crisis - assassination of Archduke Ferdinand of Austria

Outbreak of First World War, July 1914

Compare and contrast

Compare and contrast is used in texts that explicitly present similarities and differences between two or more concepts. It can also be used when students examine evidence from more than one source or make comparisons between texts or characters within stories.

Example cue words for compare and contrast	Same as, Alike, Contrasting, Different from, Similar to, Both, On the other hand, Either... or.., As well as..., As opposed to...

Venn Diagrams are frequently used to explore comparison and contrast between two or more ideas and the Double Bubble Map can also be used (see Thinking Maps p73)

In this example from a year 4 class, the students compare two characters, one from a novel they have been reading and one from a poem.

Double bubble map

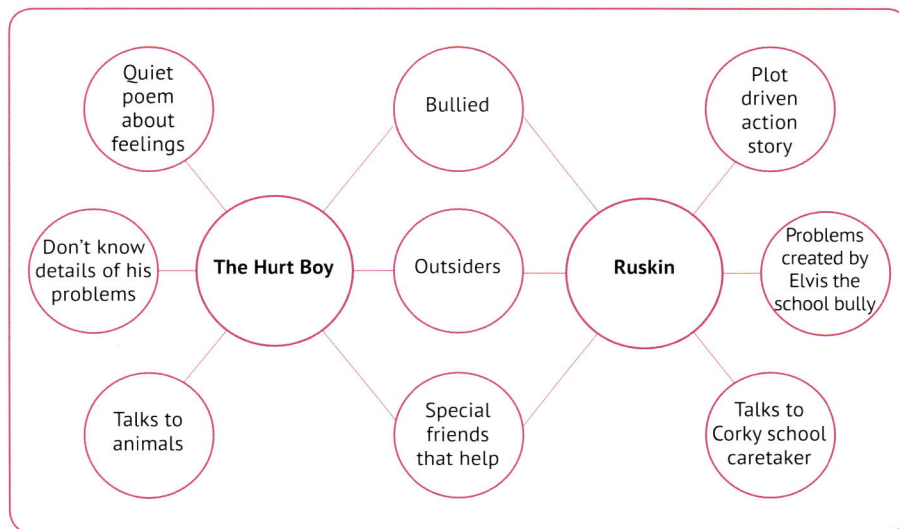

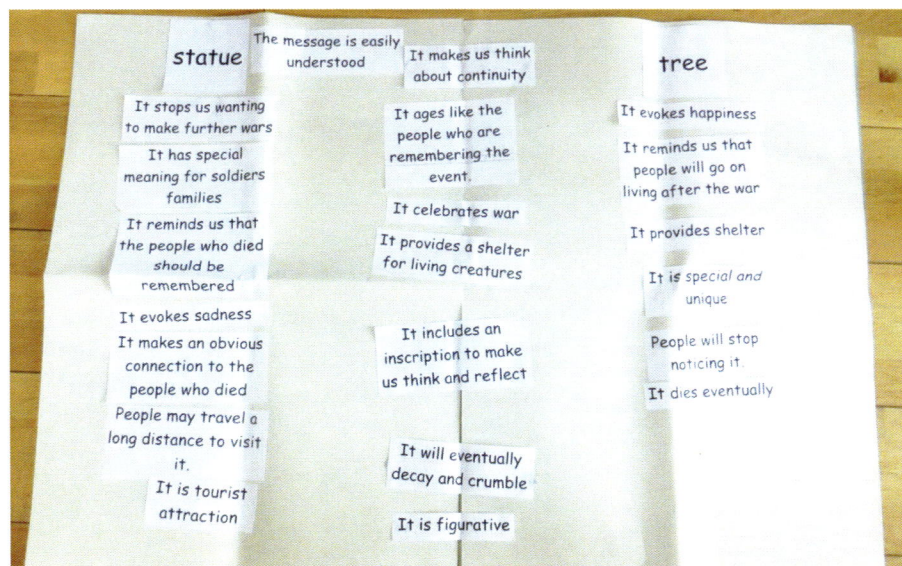

In this year 6 example from a sequence of work on Gary Crewe's *Memorial*, students have organised a set of statements into those that apply to the tree or the statue. The statements in the middle apply to both.

Graphic Representation

Problem and solution

This structure may occur in fiction or expository text. Typically, a problem is presented followed by one or more solutions. In some instances there may be an evaluation of proposed solutions followed by a suggested best solution.

Example cue words and phrases for problem and solution text structures	One reason for, A solution, For this reason, Because, This led to,

In this example a year 3 class has been reading a report about wasting energy and the steps people can take to make a difference:

Graphic solution organiser

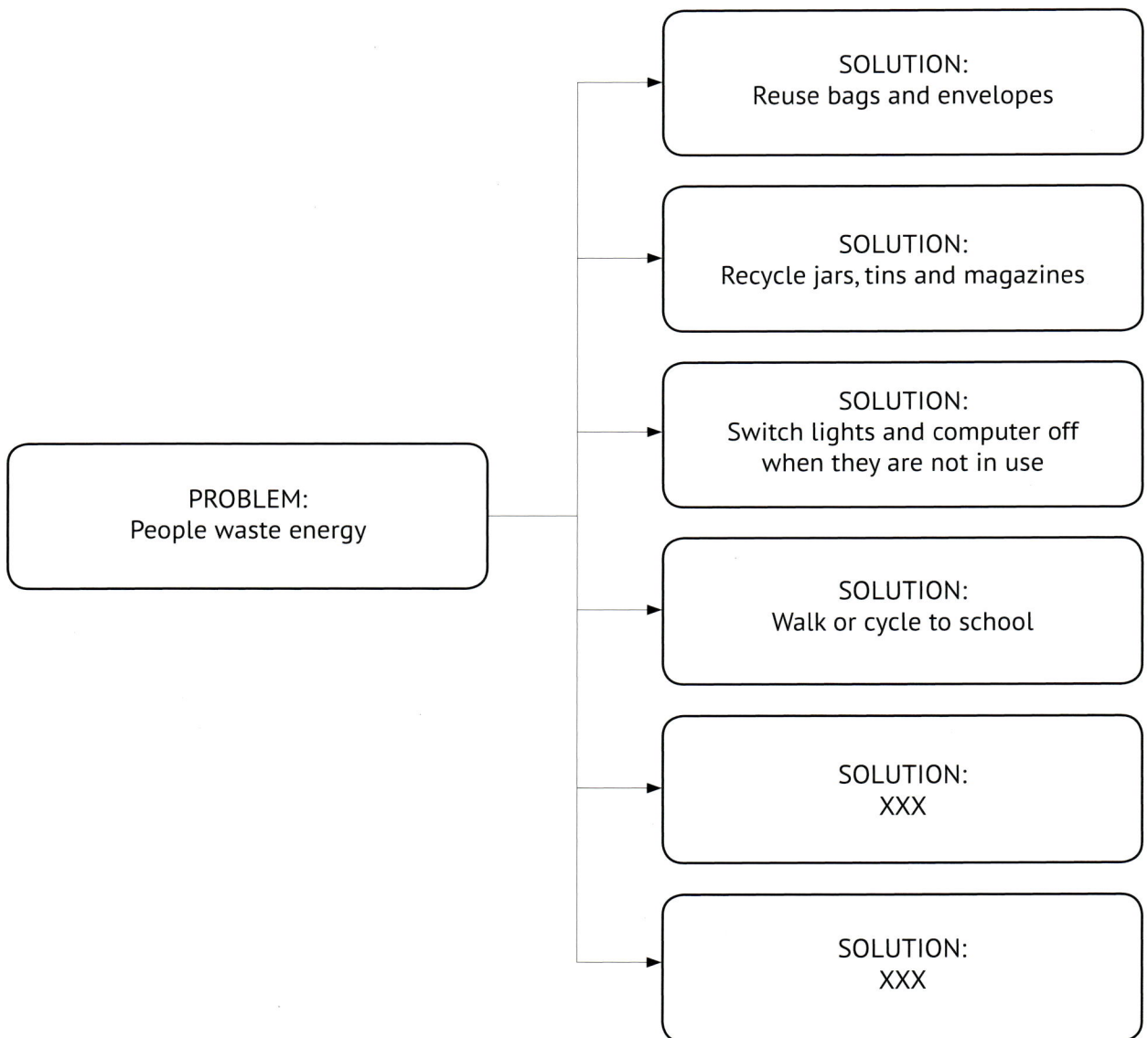

PROBLEM:
People waste energy

SOLUTION:
Reuse bags and envelopes

SOLUTION:
Recycle jars, tins and magazines

SOLUTION:
Switch lights and computer off when they are not in use

SOLUTION:
Walk or cycle to school

SOLUTION:
XXX

SOLUTION:
XXX

Graphic Representation

Question and answer

In this type of text a question is posed and then followed by answers. Questions may relate to who, what, why, where, when, how. The questions may be implied rather than explicitly stated.

Example cue words and phrases for Question and Answer text structures	How many, What, Who, How, The best estimate is…, Why, Where, When, The answer is… Given the evidence, it seems that…

T diagrams are one way to identify question and answers. One year 5 class had been studying the growth of the railways and reading a variety of sources including web based materials.

T diagram

QUESTION	ANSWER
WHO Who built the first train?	1804 Richard Trevithick built the first steam locomotive to run on rails
Who built the first railway in Britain?	Before 1840 railway lines were private and local but in 1840 …
WHAT	
WHERE Where did the first railway line run from and to?	
WHEN When was the first railway line built?	The Stockton to Darlington Railway officially opened on 27 September 1825
WHY Why was the first railway line built?	To connect the collieries in Stockton with Darlington so that coal could be transported easily.
HOW How were the railways constructed?	

Graphic Representation

Top tip for concept maps

Colours can be used to segment different branches of the concept map in order to aid memory or reinforce structure. Graphics and images might also be used, if they help to clarify or make the concept memorable.

Concept mapping

What are concept maps?

Concept maps are diagrams which help students develop their knowledge and understanding of concepts (Novak, 1990).

Why are concept maps useful?

Concept maps can be used to access prior experience and to explore and organise new information. They are characteristically hierarchical. Text (labels, items, questions) is written in boxes, which are connected using linking text to explain the relationship between them. Starting with a top down process, concept maps move from the largest concepts down to the smaller component parts. Reading the text from top to bottom creates a sentence like structure.

Concept maps:

- show organisation of concepts and ideas
- help students see relationships
- are memorable
- encourage analytical thinking
- keep learning active.

Introducing concept maps

Following the same principles as outlined previously, the teacher structures the learning to include modelling, guided practice and independent work. Initially the maps will be provisional and subject to change as more information about a concept is acquired. For this reason it is best if students are encouraged to see the initial map as draft work, using post-its that can be moved and manipulated or specially designed software such as IHMC CmapTools.

Fairy Tales: an example of a concept map used to analyse and generate discussion about genre.

This example concept map (see page 71) was created by a year 5 class as they discussed the characteristics of fairy tales prior to reading Hans Christian Andersen's *The Little Mermaid*.

The term Fairy Tale was written in a large box at the top of the diagram. The teacher introduced the topic by asking 'what do we know about fairy tales?' After a short discussion the teacher drew a second box with the linking text 'is a type of' and wrote in the second box 'short story based on a traditional folk tale' .

The students talked about the different kinds of characters that are common in fairy tales. A new branch was drawn in blue. He asked the students to write the name of characters on post-its and then place them at the end of the character branch. He then read them out: Cinderella, Woodcutter, Big Bad Wolf,

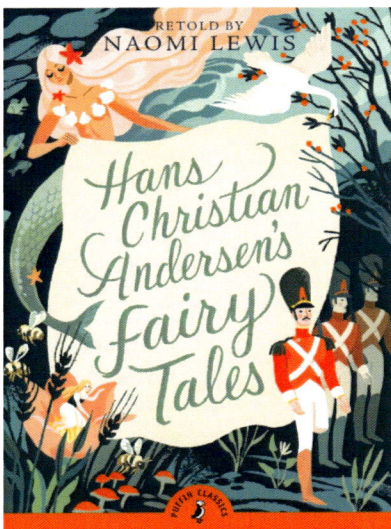

Puffin Classics

Sleeping beauty, Witch etc… and asked if there was any way that the characters might be grouped. The students decided they should be arranged as 'good characters' and 'bad characters'. Two new branches were drawn with the linking text 'sometimes the characters are', which lead to a new box 'good', and on the other branch 'sometimes the characters are' which led to the box 'bad'. Further lines were drawn with the linking text 'such as' and the students arranged their post-its appropriately at the end of the small branches.

The teacher read out the text of the map 'Fairy tales are short stories based on traditional tales. They have characters sometimes they are good such as Cinderella, Fairy Godmother, Sleeping Beauty'.

Further branches were added to the map in a similar way.

The teacher invited the students to consider whether there were any connections between the different branches. They suggested that characters made the plot happen. The teacher drew a connecting line from character to plot with the linking text 'make happen'.

After reading an unabridged version of Hans Christian Andersen's *The Little Mermaid*. The students were asked to revisit their concept map. The teacher posed the questions:

• in what ways is *The Little Mermaid* like the other fairy stories we have read?

• and in what ways do you think it is different?

• is there anything we need to change or add to our map?

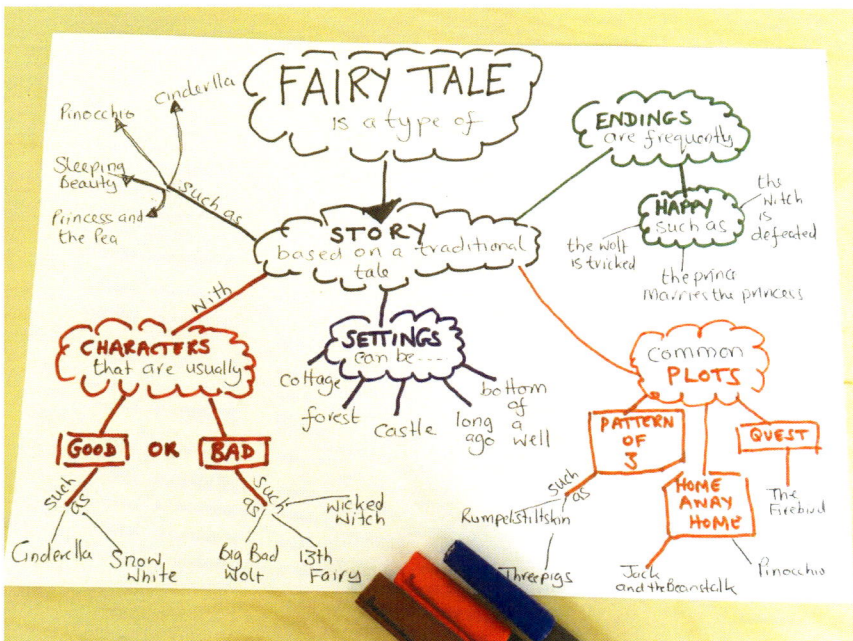

Classroom activity

Demonstrate how to construct a concept map for one of the following using the texts you are currently reading:

• A specific genre such as science fiction or mystery.

• A classification of insects.

• A scientific concept such as weather.

Model the process showing how to make links but allow the students to complete their own maps. The process is important and they need to make it their own.

• Firstly, identify the central word or concept (e.g. Fairy Tale, Insect).

• Next show how to organise the main idea into further ideas (e.g. Structure, Body). It is important to explain that this might change as more information is gathered.

• Use connecting lines or arrows to show how ideas relate to each other.

• Keep the map simple; too much information will make it too complex to map and the students may become frustrated.

• If relevant, encourage the students to draw pictures or use cut out images in addition to words.

Reflect with the students as to how the concept map can aid their understanding.

Invite students to prepare a presentation using their concept maps to help them organise their talk.

Graphic Representation

> " *As educators we are becoming more aware of the importance of children's working memory. We see that as the children become fluent with the use of thinking maps they immediately know what type thinking is required and that frees up more thinking capacity for the subject, rather than the process of recording. A further benefit is that this fluency is accompanied by a common language which children use throughout the school. Teaching time is increased because we don't need to spend as long on procedural activity.* "
>
> *Carla Ruocco, East Sheen Primary School*

Thinking maps

What are thinking maps?

Thinking maps devised by David Hyerle (2009, 2011) are a set of eight diagrams, based on eight cognitive skills. There is some discussion as to whether thinking maps are essentially different from graphic organisers. Hyerle argues that unlike graphic organisers, thinking maps are not task specific and consequently can be used more consistently to develop a common language across the school. It could be argued that this is a perceived difference which arises as much out of the misuse of graphic organisers (i.e. as pre-printed worksheets) rather than a substantive difference. However, Hyerle's identification of eight maps used to develop a common language across subjects and year groups is useful. Furthermore, as one of the schools undertaking the 4XR project had already begun a journey towards 'Thinking School' accreditation using thinking maps as one of the tools, we have outlined Hyerle's eight maps here. For further information about thinking maps, readers are directed to the publications listed at the end of this chapter.

Why are thinking maps useful?

By learning how each tool relates to a thought process students learn to independently select the maps they need and to use them inter-dependently.

Thinking maps are:

- graphically consistent

- flexible – additional bubbles can be added

- developmental – can be used at any age

- integrative – used across subjects

- reflective – students learn how to assess what they are thinking, to share responses with their peers and teachers and can amend and add as they progress.

One of the project schools was already on the journey towards becoming an accredited Thinking School and had been using the maps across the curriculum and to support writing.

The box around each of the maps is called the frame of reference. Here you record where the information comes from, e.g. reading the book, watching a video, from teachers and parents. This encourages the students to be reflective about what they are learning and consider not only WHAT they know but also HOW they know it. In terms of reading, this is an introduction to identifying sources, which older students can develop further by making judgements about reliability and validity.

Graphic Representation

The 'thinking map toolkit'.

Each of the eight maps represents a different thought process:

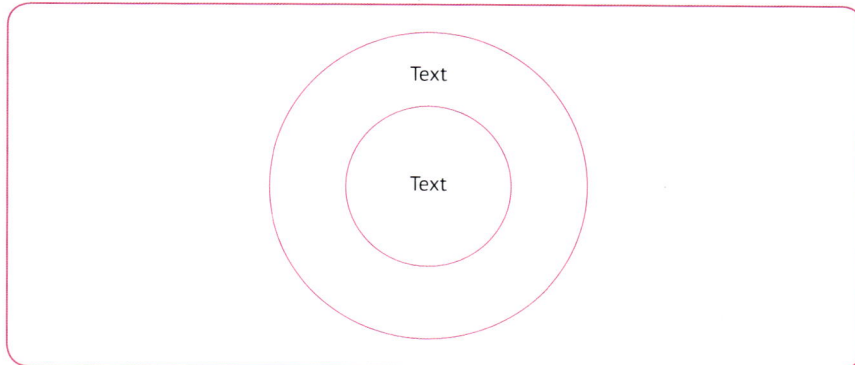

1. Circle map – defining in context. For example: in the inner circle write what you want to define – e.g. Traditional Tales. In the outer circle, record in writing or pictures everything you know about traditional tales.

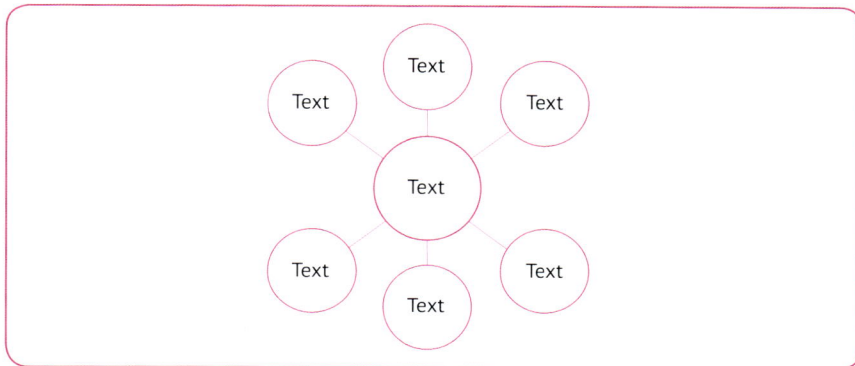

2. Bubble map – describing. For example: in the middle circle, write or draw a character you are describing. Use the outer circles to record the adjectives that describe the character.

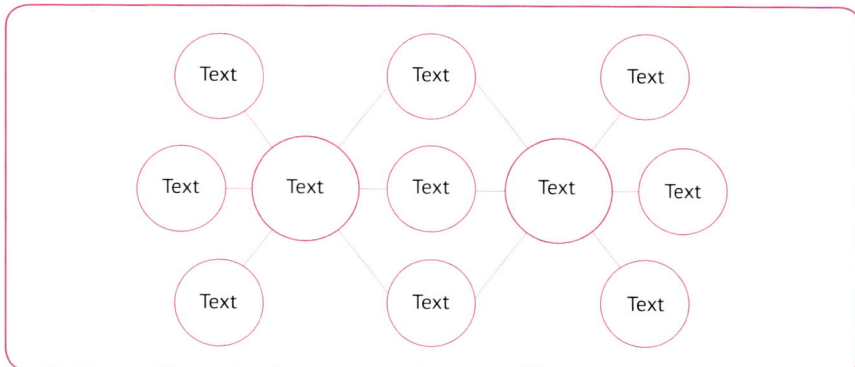

3. Double bubble map – comparing and contrasting. For example: write the names of two characters in the middle two circles. The circles (bubbles) that link to both Goldilocks and Little Red Riding Hood are for similarities. The bubbles linking to only one of the characters are for differences.

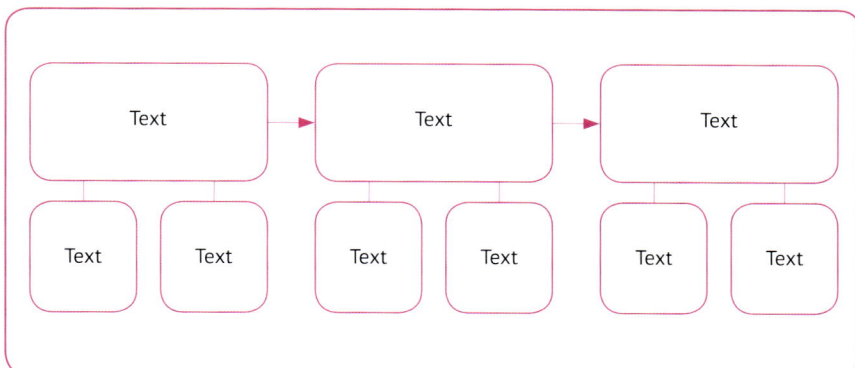

4. Flow map – sequencing. For example: Using a story, e.g. 'Little Red Riding Hood', using main boxes for students to sequence what happens in the story. The smaller boxes are for adding additional information, perhaps targeting students to find or describe how the characters are feeling or to identify time connectives.

73

Graphic Representation

The 'thinking map toolkit' (continued)

5. Multi-flow map – cause and effect. For example: *Romeo and Juliet*; the map can be used to identify the cause and effects of the different events in this story.

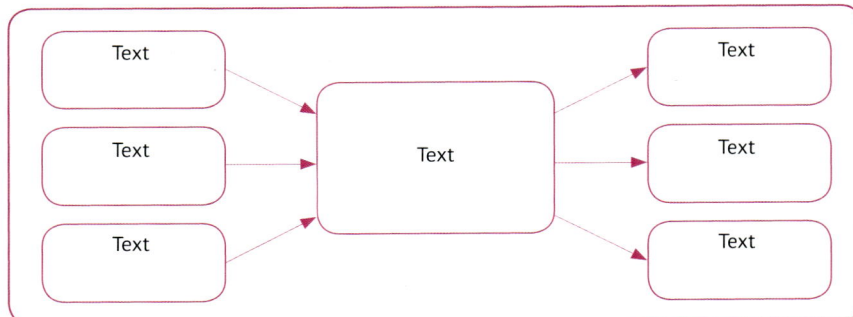

| Text |
| Text |
| Text |

Text

| Text |
| Text |
| Text |

6. Tree map – classifying. For example: identifying different themes within a story.

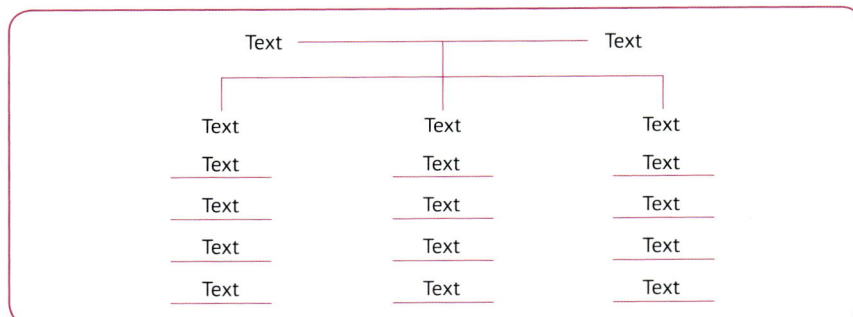

Text — Text

Text Text Text
Text Text Text
Text Text Text
Text Text Text
Text Text Text

7. Brace map – whole parts. For example, identifying the parts of a story: beginning, middle and end. And then breaking down each part into further components e.g. what makes up the beginning of a story.

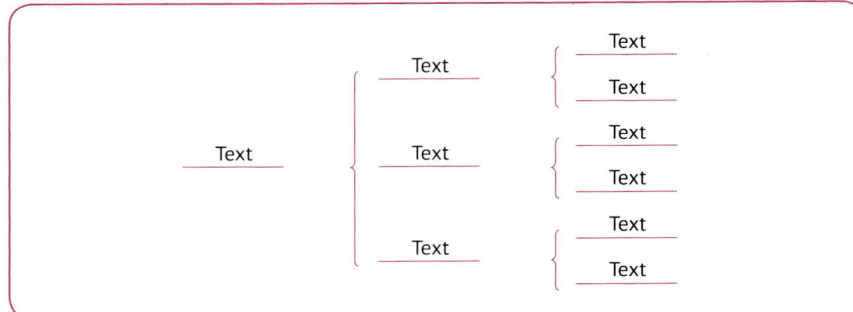

Text

Text
Text
Text

Text
Text
Text
Text
Text
Text

8. Bridge map – seeing analogies. For example, looking at the relating factor of the villain in traditional tales.

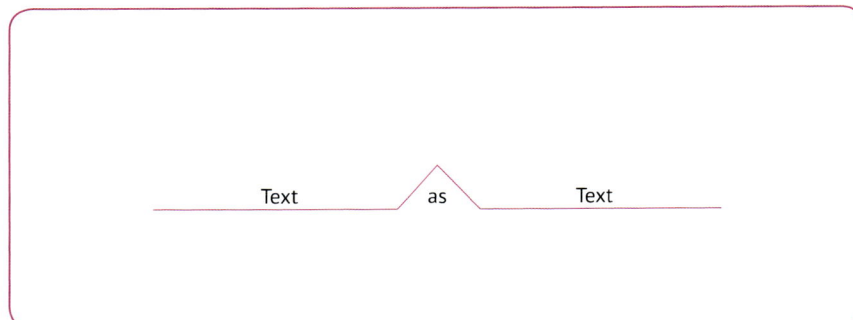

Text — as — Text

Using thinking maps in context: a teaching sequence

One of the principles for using thinking maps is that they can be used in concert to help build understanding. In this sequence, Carla Ruocco and Debbie Caner worked with a number of maps to support a year 6 group of high attaining readers.

To begin the students were given a picture book *Memorial* by Gary Crew and illustrated by Shaun Tan to read independently for homework. This time, for students to read independently and to begin to form thoughts and ideas, was considered an important part of the process.

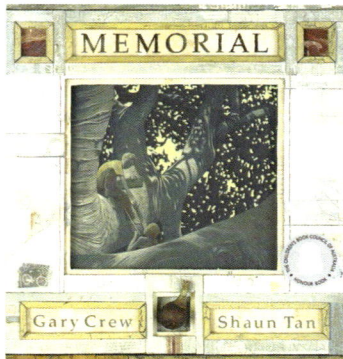

Memorial tells the story of a tree planted beside a statue of the unknown soldier at the end of the First World War. Years on, the tree has grown large and unruly, threatening to dislodge the statue and damage the road. Four generations reflect on what the tree has meant to them and the council's proposal to cut the tree down.

Hodder Children's Books

Recording ideas and first responses: using the circle map

After reading the students recorded their initial responses on a circle map. They noted their first impressions, any questions they had about the text and anything they found strange or puzzling. The completed maps were brought to a guided reading session and used to initiate discussion. The students shared their first thoughts and their maps.

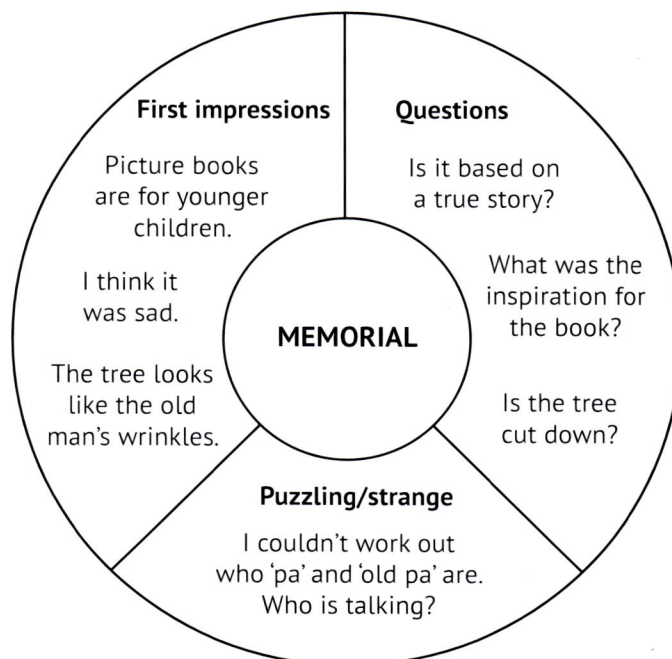

First impressions

Picture books are for younger children.

I think it was sad.

The tree looks like the old man's wrinkles.

Questions

Is it based on a true story?

What was the inspiration for the book?

Is the tree cut down?

MEMORIAL

Puzzling/strange

I couldn't work out who 'pa' and 'old pa' are. Who is talking?

Graphic Representation

Taking it deeper, revisiting the text: adding to maps

The students reviewed the book page by page, moving on when there was a general consensus that they had fully explored their ideas. The students studied the pictures and the text, noticing details that had passed them by on the first reading. They were encouraged to add to their circle maps with any new questions or thoughts. By using different colours for writing in the second session it was clear how the students' understanding developed as a result of the guided lesson.

Revisiting the text is an important part of the process; it allows students to build on the ideas that they have started to formulate as well as self-check any confusions or find answers to their own questions. There can be a tendency to move quickly from one text to the next, but consequently opportunities for deeper learning can be lost.

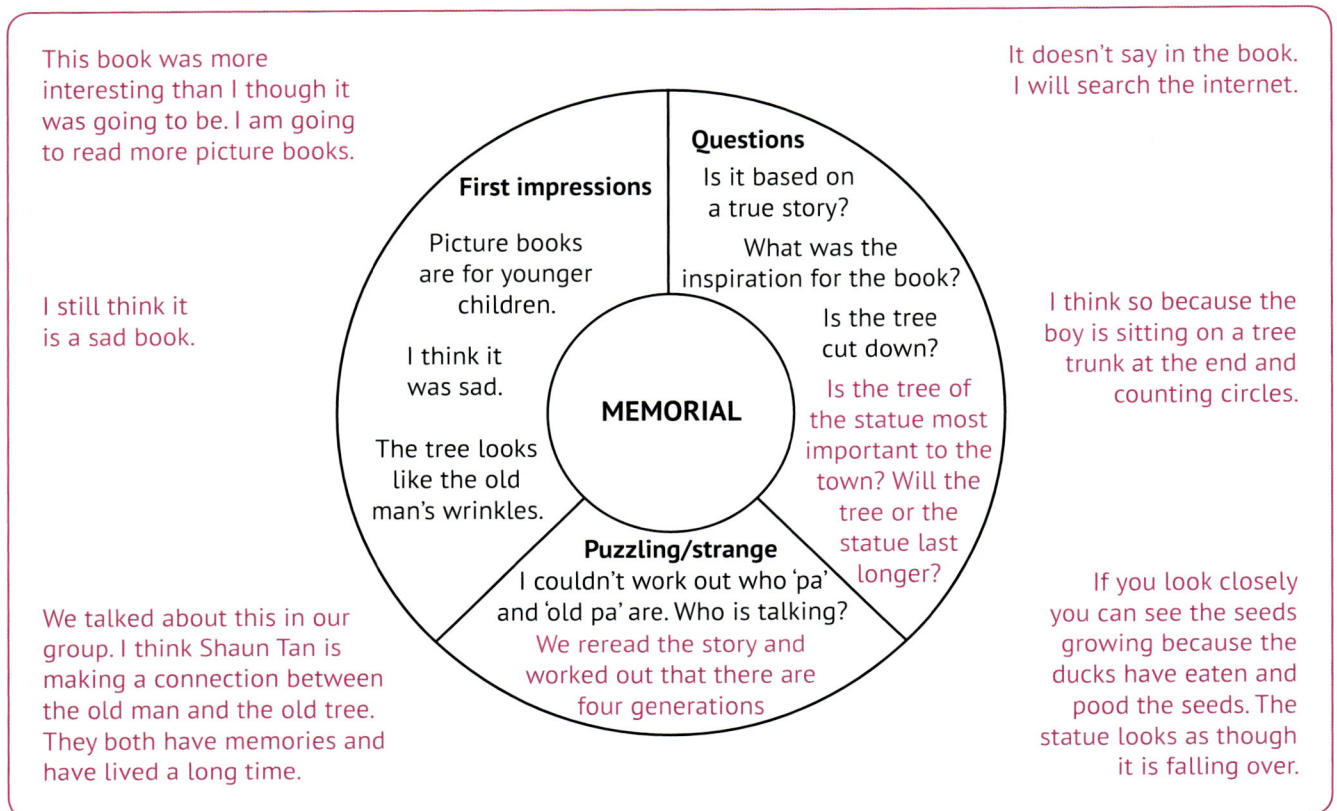

This book was more interesting than I though it was going to be. I am going to read more picture books.

It doesn't say in the book. I will search the internet.

First impressions

Questions

Is it based on a true story?

What was the inspiration for the book?

Is the tree cut down?

Picture books are for younger children.

I think it was sad.

MEMORIAL

Is the tree of the statue most important to the town? Will the tree or the statue last longer?

I still think it is a sad book.

I think so because the boy is sitting on a tree trunk at the end and counting circles.

The tree looks like the old man's wrinkles.

Puzzling/strange

I couldn't work out who 'pa' and 'old pa' are. Who is talking?

We reread the story and worked out that there are four generations

We talked about this in our group. I think Shaun Tan is making a connection between the old man and the old tree. They both have memories and have lived a long time.

If you look closely you can see the seeds growing because the ducks have eaten and pood the seeds. The statue looks as though it is falling over.

Expanding thinking

The role of the teacher in supporting the development of reading comprehension is to work with students' current understandings and move their thinking forward. The teacher scaffolds with prompts and questions that enable students to make connections, probe and extend their ideas, make their thinking explicit, justify their opinions and increase metacognition.

At the end of the previous session the students had posed a question about the whether the tree or the statue was the most important memorial.

To help the students answer the question they used a double bubble map to compare and contrast the two symbols. The map helped them to organise their thoughts.

The teacher assembled the group and asked them to present their ideas. In making their points, they were asked to give a well-reasoned response, even though their answers differed from each other.

At the end of the session the students were asked to summarise their understanding of the story and review their circle maps to see if there were any unanswered questions. This revealed that the students' comprehension had deepened and also served as an assessment to see where this could be taken in the following session.

Comparing texts

To synthesise their understanding of *Memorial*, the students completed a tree diagram showing the themes that they had identified in their discussion. They then read a short story by David Almond, '*A World With No War*', which the teacher had selected on the grounds of thematic similarity. After reading and discussing, the students completed a second tree diagram showing the themes in the short story. The two diagrams where then used as a means of comparing the stories and extending their thinking to consider the different treatment of the themes by the authors/illustrator.

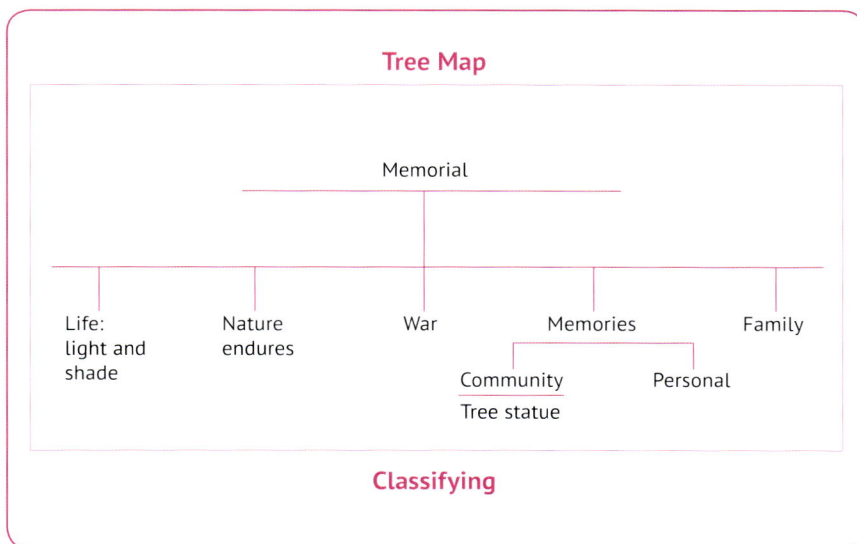

Tree Map

Memorial

| Life: light and shade | Nature endures | War | Memories | Family |

Community — Personal
Tree statue

Classifying

Walker Books

Further Reading

Hyerle, D.N. (2009) *Visual Tools for Transforming Knowledge into Information* London: Sage

Hyerle, D.N (2011) *Student Successes with Thinking Maps* London: Sage

Jiang, X. & Grabe, W (2007) *Graphic Organisers in reading instruction: research findings and issues in* Reading as a Foreign Language *19, 1: 34-55*

Novak, J. D. (1990). *Concept maps and Venn diagrams: Two metacognitive tools for science and mathematics education.* Instructional Science, *19: 29-52.*

Petty, G (2009) *Evidence Based Teaching a practical approach* Oxford: Nelson Thornes

Zwaan R.A. (1994) *Effects of genre expectations on text comprehension in* Journal of Experimental Psychology *Learning, Memory, Cognition 20: 920-33*

CMap tools for iPAD

Summary

At the end of the session the teachers noted 'We were very impressed with how, in completing the map, the discussion was focused and channelled. The students were able to identify the themes and justify their thoughts. They also recognised the similarities with *Memorial* and made other connections with other familiar texts such as *Romeo and Juliet*.'

The teachers observed:

- there was far less teacher talk than usual

- the students were able to reflect more on their own responses and to make connections with their experiences and other texts

- the students listened attentively to each other's ideas

- they raised their own questions as they were confronted with different ways of thinking about the text

- discussion was focussed and not artificially constraining.

Students commented that:

- thinking maps had helped them explain their thinking about challenging texts

- maps would enable them to learn more independently in their reading groups.

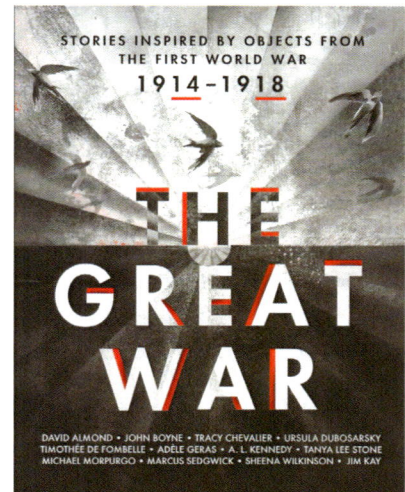

STRATEGIES

Reading Audit: Resources and Environment

School: **Date:**

Organisation of resources	Comments	Classroom	Library
Are texts accessible through appropriate shelving?			
Texts clearly signposted for easy access? How do students locate fiction texts? How do students locate non-fiction texts?			
Are book displays varied and interesting e.g. topic, theme, author?			
How frequently can students access the resources e.g. all the time, timetabled session, infrequently?			
Is there a designated place for pupil-to-pupil book recommendations?			
Are there engaging reading challenges available for the students to try?			
Are there recommendations which are changed frequently e.g. 'Top 10 Mystery Stories' style posters?			
Are students involved in the organisation and maintenance of the resources?			
Are governors/parents active in the upkeep of the resources?			
Is there a library management system in place e.g. Junior Librarian?			

Reading Areas	Comments	Classroom	Library
Are there different styles of seating to suit different purposes e.g. chairs, tables, armchairs, beanbags, sofas?			
Storyteller chair?			
Is the décor welcoming and appealing e.g. colours carpets, plants, drapes?			
Are books promoted and attractively displayed?			
Is the area tidy and generally inviting?			
Is there a notice board area and/or flipchart and pens for pupil-to-pupil communication or adult to pupil communication?			
Pupil book review journal accessible?			
Is the book stock up-to-date and are old worn copies discarded and replaced regularly?			
Multiple sets of books for guided or group reading available at times outside of these sessions?			

Reading Audit: Resources and Environment

School: **Date:**

Range of Genre and Format	Comments (Consider 6UP level suitability throughout)	Classroom	Library
Are the texts suited to the attainment and the interests of the students?			
Are texts in the classroom changed regularly e.g. once a term so that students always have fresh and inspiring material?			
Are the following available? • Classic fiction and poetry e.g. Charles Dickens, Lewis Carroll, Edith Nesbit, J. R. R.Tolkien, Robert Louis Stevenson			
• Classic fiction adaptations, sequels and modern versions			
• Historical fiction			
• Science fiction			
• Mystery			
• Adventure			
• Myths and legends			
• Comedy			
• Thriller			
• Fantasy			
• Ghost stories and suspense			
• Short story collections			
• Traditional tales			
• Graphic novels			
• Picture books (including picture books for older readers)			
• Comics			
• Stories representing a wide range of cultures			
• Plays, including Shakespeare			
• Single poet collections			
• Poetry anthologies			
• Thematic collections			
• Non-fiction to support curriculum topics			
• Non-fiction to support reading for pleasure			

Reading Audit: Resources and Environment

School: **Date:**

Library and book purchasing policy	Comments	Classroom	Library
Development and responsibility			
Is the management and maintenance of the library under regular review?			
Is there a designated lead or team responsible for overseeing the development of the library?			
Book purchasing			
Is there an annual budget for replenishment and purchasing new books and resources?			
Who choses stock? Library lead? Teachers? Students?			
Is the budget reliant on fundraising and parent involvement?			
Who manages the budget?			
Does book selection take into account wider reader beyond curriculum topics and students' reading interests?			
Staffing and access			
Who staffs the library?			
When is the library open? Timetabled lessons, lunchtimes, after school, before school?			
Library and classroom collections			
Is there a regular exchange of stock between the library and class collections?			

Reading Audit: Resources and Environment

School: **Date:**

Range of genre and format	Comments (Consider 6UP level suitability throughout)	Classroom	Library
• Dual language books/ MFL			
• Autobiography/biography			
• Students' newspapers and magazine e.g. *First News, The Buzz*			
• Students' published texts			
• Higher level dictionaries, appropriate to texts read			
• Other collections available e.g. books by the same author, books in a series			
• Talking texts (via earphones)			
• Computers/ laptops/ipads			
• Display of recommended web links appropriate to a topic area, theme, author or poet			
• Email facilities e.g. inter-school			
• Collection of appropriate film texts - fiction			
• Collection of appropriate film texts – non-fiction			
• Espresso or similar subject-based, multi-media information software			

Reading to the class	Comments	Classroom	Library
Do teachers regularly read aloud to the class?			
Are choices varied and age appropriate?			
Are students introduced to the best contemporary and classic authors?			
Is there a balance between reading familiar favourites and widening students' reading horizons?			
Guided and group reading			
Are the resources well managed and accessible?			
Are they well used? If not, what is the reason e.g. are they too long, insufficiently interesting or challenging?			
Are the following available in group sets: • short story collections • poetry collections • high quality picture books for older readers • real world texts • high quality non-fiction • shorter novels e.g. Philip Pullman *Clockwork*, Frank Cottrell Boyce *The Unforgotten Coat*			

Student Perception Scale

	Strongly agree	Agree	Undecided	Disagree	Strongly disagree
I think that I am a good reader					
My teacher thinks my reading is good					
I understand what I am reading better than most of the other students in my class					
I like finding new words when I am reading					
I like reading fiction					
I feel happy when I am reading					
I know the meanings of more words than most students of my age					
I like to talk about the book I am reading					
I always understand what I am reading					
I think reading is relaxing					
I read more than most students					
I enjoy factual books					
People in my family think I am a good reader					
I always choose my own books					
I recognise more words than I used to					
I read more than I used to					
Students in my class think I have good ideas about the book we are reading					
I feel intelligent when I am reading					
I like reading poetry					
My teacher listens to my ideas					
I am getting better at reading					
I feel comfortable when I am reading					
I read faster than I used to					
I enjoy reading aloud in class					
I understand what I read better than I could before					
When I read, I need less help than I used to					
When I am reading, I feel calm					
Other students think I am a good reader					

Student Reading Interests and Preferences

Which of the following do you read outside of school more than once a month?

(You may tick more than one box)

Websites (general)	
Blogging/networking websites (such as Facebook, Tumblr, Instagram, Twitter)	
Newspapers	
Magazines	
Graphic novels or comics	
Emails	
Fiction books	
Poetry	
Factual books	
Manuals/instructions	
None of these	

How often do you read outside of school? (Tick one box only)

Every day or almost every day	
Once or twice a week	
Once or twice a month	
Never or almost never	

Which of the following do the adults at home encourage you to read?

(You may tick more than one box)

Websites (general)	
Blogging/networking websites (such as Facebook, Tumblr, Instagram, Twitter)	
Newspapers	
Magazines	
Graphic novels or comics	
Emails	
Fiction books	
Poetry	
Factual books	
Manuals/instructions	
None of these	

Student Reading Interests and Preferences

Which of the following does your teacher encourage you to read at school?
(You may tick more than one box)

Websites (general)	
Blogging/networking websites (such as Facebook, Tumblr, Instagram, Twitter)	
Newspapers	
Magazines	
Graphic novels or comics	
Emails	
Fiction books	
Poetry	
Factual books	
Manuals/instructions	
None of these	

Can you find what you want to read at home? (tick only one box)

Yes	
No	

Can you find what you want to read at school? (tick only one box)

Yes	
No	

Do you visit the public library? (tick only one box)

Yes	
No	

Do you prefer reading at school or at home? (tick one box only)

School	
Home	

Student Reading Interests and Preferences

In a few words, tell us why you prefer reading at home or at school?

Question Quadrant

Photocopy onto A3 or reproduce on a large A1 sheet of paper

	Answer not found in the text	
Answer found in the text		
	Question has one answer	**Question has more than one answer**

Finding a Theme

Book title:

Characters	Setting	Problem

Summary: Who? Where? Main events?

A lesson learned by a character (review characters, problem, and summary)	THEME - the big idea
Character name: **Lesson learned:**	

What's the Big Idea?

Book title:

Big idea or topic:

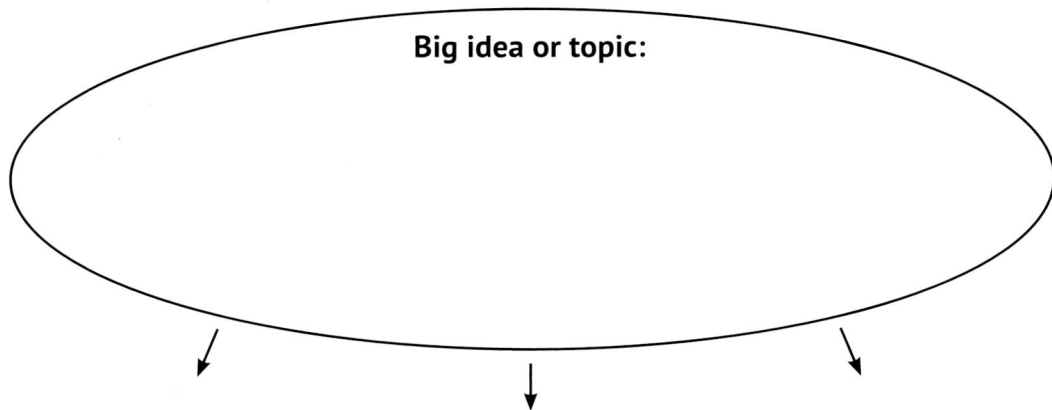

What characters say and do that demonstrate this:		

What is learned?

THEME - the big idea

Problem - Solution Organiser (version 1)

Book title:

Problems

Solutions

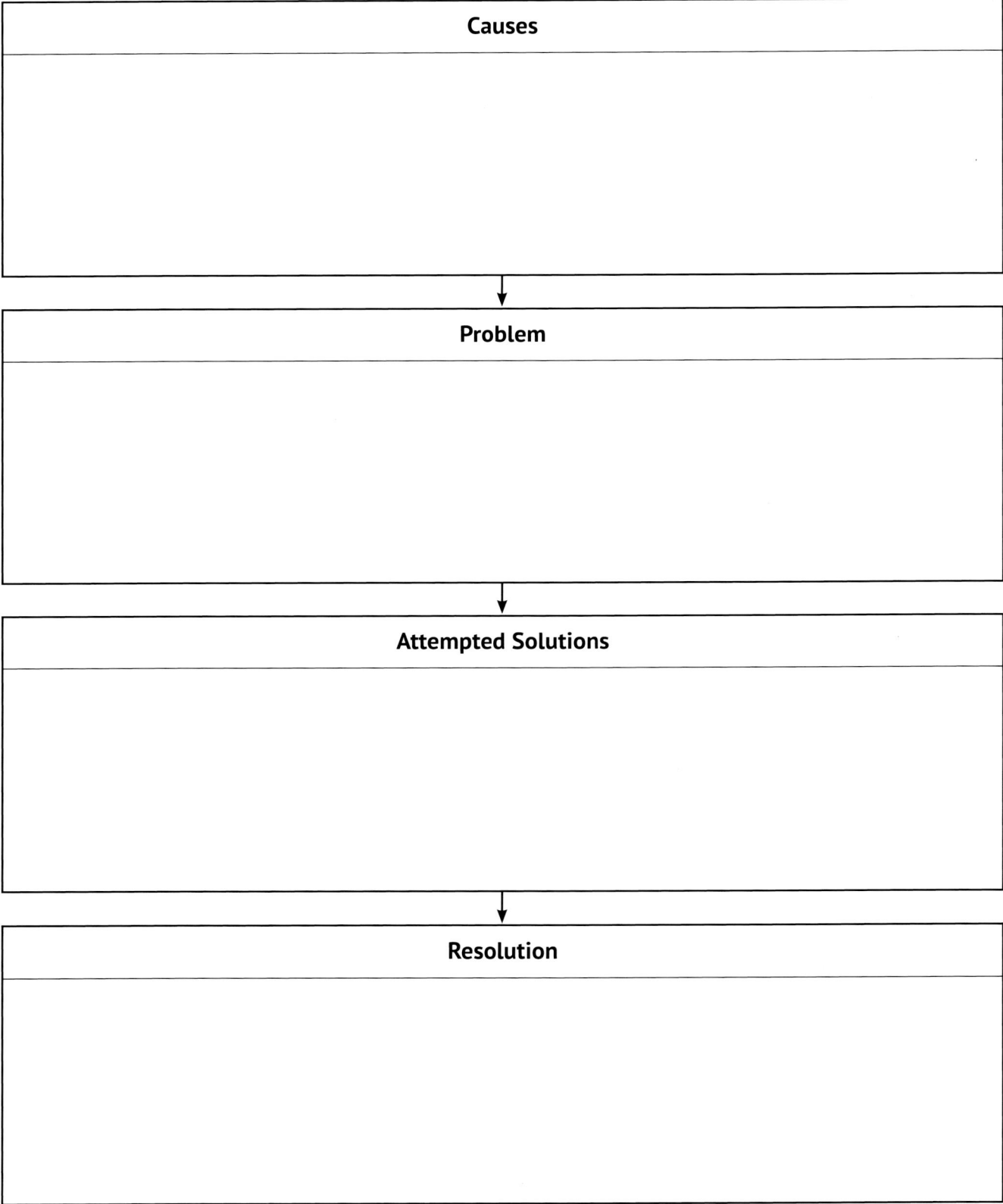

Problem - Solution Organiser (version 2)

Book title:

Causes

↓

Problem

↓

Attempted Solutions

↓

Resolution

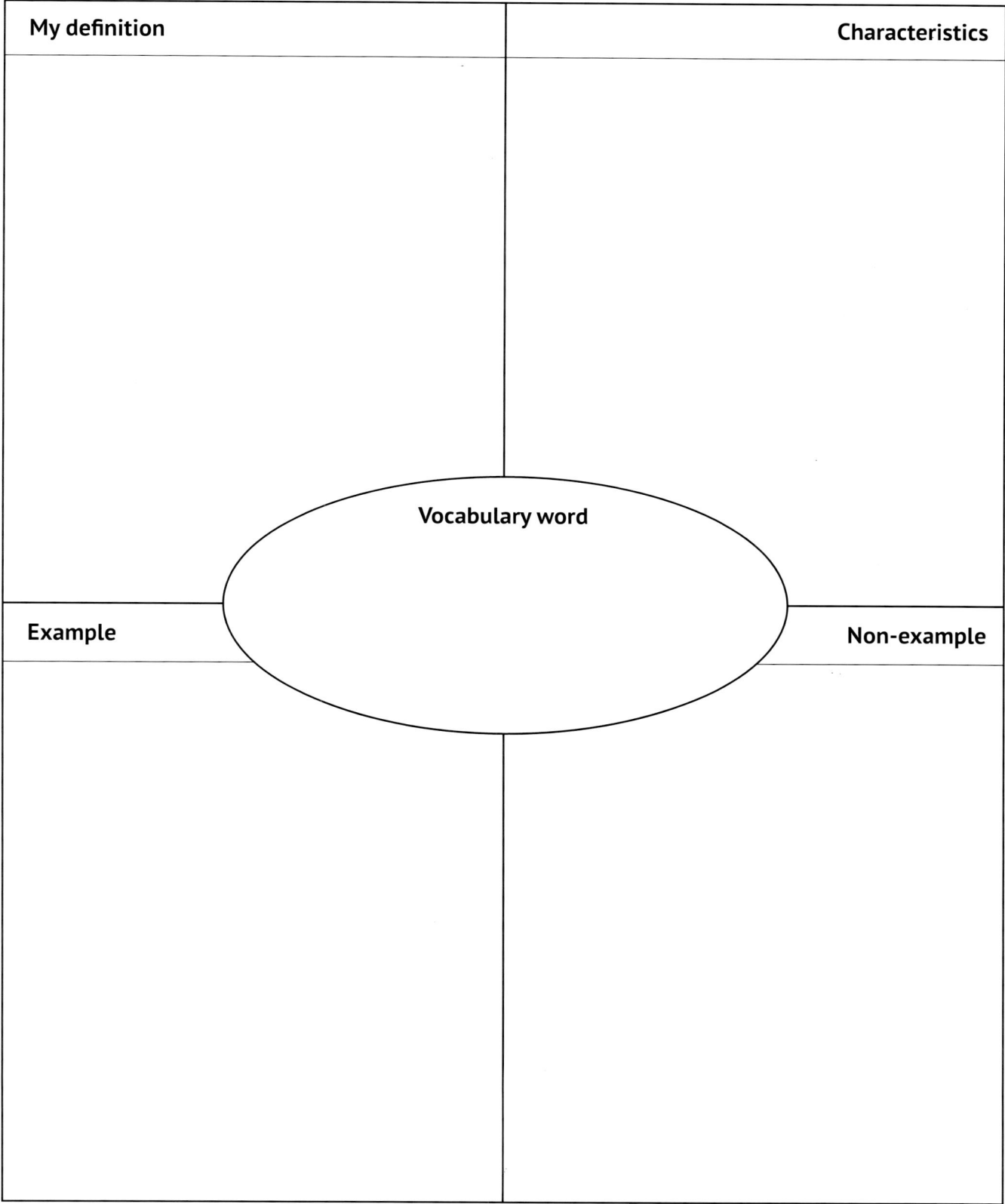

Freyer Diagram

Book title:

My definition	Characteristics

Vocabulary word

Example	Non-example

Vocabulary Journal

Book title:

Target Word	How is it used in the text?	What clues to the meaning can you work out?	Where have you seen or heard this word before?	Dictionary definitions (use more than one dictionary)	Homework: new examples and quotations

Book title:

This text reminds me of...

TEXT	**My experiences ...**	**SELF**
TEXT	**Books I have read or films I have seen ...**	**TEXT**
TEXT	**Big ideas, themes, related to the world ...**	**WORLD**

Writing a Summary (Fiction)

Book title:

Somebody ... Who is the main character?	
Wanted ... What did the character want?	
But ... What was the problem?	
So ... How did the character over come the problem?	
Then ... What was the resolution to the story?	

Now write your summary ...

Writing a Summary (Fiction)

Book title:

Now write your summary (cont.)

The website accompanying this handbook provides video exemplification of learning and teaching. Further examples will be added periodically, so do revisit to see find out what has been happening in the world of 4XR.

Questions can be submitted via the website and we are keen to hear from teachers who are working with these materials in schools or who are interested in developing the work with us.

www.4XR.uk